ARE WE DOOMED?

EXPLORING RELATIONSHIPS
BETWEEN
THE 60S COUNTERCULTURE
AND OUR
21ST CENTURY

CHRIS JARMAIN

Copyright © All rights reserved. No part of this publication may be reproduced, distributed, or transmitted in any form or by any means without the prior written permission of the publisher, except in the case of brief quotations embodied in critical reviews and certain other non-commercial uses permitted by copyright law.

Contents

Introduction..v

Chapter 1 - How did the counterculture begin?.......................1

Chapter 2 - The Civil Rights Movement....................................27

Chapter 3 - The Gay Liberation Movement..............................45

Chapter 4 - The Human Potential Movement..........................53

Chapter 5 - Psychology and spirituality.....................................59

Chapter 6 - Psychedelics, LSD and conscious awareness.......73

Chapter 7 - The 'Happening', society and the Summer Of Love, 1967..85

Chapter 8 - A symbol of peace, the Hippie peace sign ☮........97

Chapter 9 - A coming end to the 60s counterculture............105

Chapter 10 - What about today though?................................115

Chapter 11 - What is the mind-set of the younger generation today?..135

Chapter 12 - Are we Doomed?
The issues of society and the directions we are headed....................151

Chapter 13 - Bloomer, 60s philosophy and fixing our social issues....179

Introduction

What is a counterculture?

A counterculture is a new found way of living, or a lifestyle with attitudes opposed to or an altered variation of the prevailing social norms. Typically arisen by idealists and or visionaries.

How did we get here?

Have you ever looked at the world around you and asked yourself "How did we get here?" How fascinating is it that our society is so diverse, varied, outrageous and at times extreme? Today, I wonder, what if the Hippies actually managed to destroy our society, instead of healing it or spreading peace within it? Are we now unable to find meaning, value and fulfilment within our 21st century because of the 60s counterculture? Has what we now consider to be 'their' counterculture removed 'our' chances of hope, but instead created a world of doom? This is a rather cynical opinion to hold in retrospect of a loving, peace filled counterculture, but after all is said and done, is peace actually an illusion? Hopefully, we might have some answers by the end of this book, but in all honesty: Are We Doomed?

    This being said, I often look back in time whilst I'm playing music from the past, all the great events from the 60s come to mind. I imagine how fun, wild and exciting it would be if I was actually there.

As the slogan goes; "Sex, Drugs and Rock n Roll", an almost teenage utopia, I was certainly entertained by this utopian idea when I was a teenager myself. So, today, it is time I welcome you to join me on this fascinating voyage to the 60s era, possibly I'm not the only one who has a profound sense of being oddly connected to an era I wasn't even born in. Part of me believes the 60s is still relevant today, even though many things have evolved and changed with time. Like I was saying at the beginning, our world today just seems outrageous!?

Sadly, a cultural shift has been occurring over the past 20 years known as the Doomer, the Doomer Generation or Doomerism. This philosophical worldview will be explored as it seems rather extreme and rather unsettling, or is it actually that extreme? Does the 60s counterculture have any links or answers as to why over 50% of our younger generation today identify with this Doomed outlook? Find out with me in this enlightening study of our culture today, whilst we look back at how it all began. What did the counterculture stand for then, and what does it still stand for now?! I invite you to join me as we start exploring relationships between the 60s counterculture and our 21st century. Are you ready?

You can also find a 5hr+ playlist on Spotify showcasing the songs referenced throughout this book. The playlist has the same name as the book title.

https://open.spotify.com/playlist/7lGEiYhbKkrS40N41FlBHz?si=Hu3pdOPTRN2twbNv5tVNGw

Chapter 1

How did the counterculture begin?

Through the 40s, 50s, 60s and 70s a movement involving the younger generation, mainly based around the Western hemisphere began rejecting the social norms. The generation typically associated with this 60s era is known as the "Baby Boomers".

The generally accepted concept is that the 60s counterculture movement began in America. Most of the issues were felt more strongly here than in other places throughout the world, although it didn't take long for everyone else to soon catch up. I will list key aspects of the 60s counterculture movement throughout this chapter and through the next few chapters.

Why the name Baby Boomers?

The generation born at this time is referred to as the 'Baby Boomers', 'Boomer Generation' or simply 'Boomer'. This name is due to a 'Boom' in births occurring, again largely in the Western hemisphere, between 1946 and 1964. This was in part due to a new found confidence and a new found sense of security following the economic hardship, and uncertainties of the Great Depression, followed then by WW2, which came and went. These changes allowed people to feel freer after the pressures began to be lifted and left behind. People started having children more easily and as a result the birth rates 'boomed'.

The Boomer Generation began in 1946, just after WW2 had ended. Many people either knowingly or unknowingly saw this post war era as a new beginning for humanity. People were able to see the world in a new, raw and unfiltered way. But it opened people up to the sensitivity of the situation, creating a need for social change. No longer are the down trodden of society going to be treated the way they had been in the past, especially after what had happened during these two world wars. After all, this was now a new era of humanity, so, let's act like it!

The first issue I find with this mind-set is that it splits our timeline into two. The history prior to the events of World War 2 is almost seen as irrelevant, thus many who come across history as a subject may find it difficult to see beyond World War 2 itself. By seeing the 20th century as a new era entirely, you tend to blind yourself from seeing anything past or beyond it. Anything that happens within this 'new era' automatically becomes 'special' or holds more weight than it probably deserves. This might be why the war in Vietnam was seen as so 'outrageous'. Our trend of being ignorant of our history before World War 2 in general today is likely a hangover of the counterculture of the 1960s. Perhaps this theory of the counterculture holding this narrative towards society is a new one for you? But you might ask "Why, or how did the counterculture have such an effect if this really is the case?", well I hope to elaborate on this 'why' question throughout this book. I hope to identify many more positive and negative aspects like this throughout the book. Perhaps this trend of seeing our time frame as 'THE' only time frame that matters has stuck around? What do you think or feel?

Although many people associate the 60s counterculture with the Boomer generation, this isn't entirely correct. Many who were born during the later half of the Boomer generation would not have been old enough to have been involved in the many celebrated aspects of the 60s. The generation prior to the Boomers was known as "The Silent Generation", this generation is typically defined as people who were born from 1928 to 1945. However, this earlier generation has been noted as forming the leadership of the civil rights movement, the 1960s counterculture and also for creating the rock and roll music of the 1950s and 1960s.

Some notable figures who shaped the 60s counterculture who were born in this generational cohort were; Bob Dylan, all the band members from The Beatles, Martin Luther King Jr, Jimi Hendrix and Janis Joplin to name a few.

The name "Silent Generation" is characterized as people who were trending towards conformity and traditionalism. A magazine called Time published an article in 1951 that had this to say:

"The most startling fact about the younger generation is its silence. With some rare exceptions, youth is nowhere near the rostrum. By comparison with the Flaming Youth of their fathers & mothers, today's younger generation is a still, small flame. It does not issue manifestoes, make speeches or carry posters. It has been called the "Silent Generation."

I find in retrospect that this was an understatement, because many people who advocated for direct change were born during the Silent Generation, such figures as Martin Luther King Jr are a leading example here.

In essence, the Baby Boomers are still considered to be 'the' generation that made the change, but with this insight now, it was actually an eclectic mix of both the Silent and Boomer Generation who made 'the' changes.

The American Dream

Before the 1950s, a phrase and set of ideals was called "The American Dream" This was in reference to social norms or perhaps better put social ideals. In part, one of these social norms meant women were to stay at home and become a housewives, who cared for the children, cooked the meals and cleaned the house. Women could have a difficult time entering into some higher education establishments, they had fears of discrimination against them if they did. As a result, women couldn't enter into some job roles due to a very male dominated platform. Due to this 'American dream' women could be seen as just the stereotypical housewife, and nothing more.

On the other hand, men were expected to have a decent education, find a steady job and essentially become the provider for their home and family. This caused a huge rise in consumerism as a result. The consumer market was largely based on people's colour and targeted its audience in response to this.

This formation of society was the foundation to work from and to aim for, it caused a lot of social unrest for the new Boomer Generation. A large number of younger people felt they didn't have to live in this way, nor did they want to because of the many faults and issues they felt it had. The younger generation began to question and challenge these ideals, creating new ideals that had creative ways of thinking instead. A counterculture therefore began to bubble up.

Another social norm at the time included the "Jim Crow Law". This law meant it was legal for racial segregation. The law was enforced around the late 19th century and early 20th century. A seemingly well established law by the time the Boomer Generation was born.

'Jim Crow was a term used to denote an African American citizen'.

Due to these notable social disadvantages and issues with many more not currently mentioned here, a counterculture unsurprisingly began to arise. The beginning of this counterculture beacon was held high by the Beat movement. But the Beatniks weren't the first ones...

The first post war youth culture

Those who have studied American culture would likely say the Beatniks preceded the Hippies. But in the United Kingdom this wasn't entirely the case. The first UK youth culture to be depicted as a youth culture by news articles, and by general pop culture were the Ted's or Teddy boys. During the 50s in the UK, by the middle of the decade, a certain style was forming, one that encapsulated 'Edwardian' drape jackets, crepe-soled 'brothel creeper' shoes, cowboy-style bootlace ties, and elaborate quiff hairstyles. Due to their aesthetics, you could say they were a throwback culture, and I say this to mean the Teds held onto older styles and values of UK culture.

The youth culture was mostly recognised in conjunction with Rock and Roll music, and a result of the rioting that accompanied the release of the film 'Rock Around the Clock' in 1956, by Bill Hayley and his comets.

Scholars today depict the Teds as a mostly working class youth culture, due to their antics and social behaviours. But as time drifted along from the 50s into the 60s in the UK, a new type of middle class culture was beginning to come through. This was the Beatniks or Beat Generation. The Beatniks didn't form out of the Teds, the beat movement was largely inspired by the American sub culture of the 40s and 50s. It is just that the UK lags behind the Americans for various reasons.

Who were the Beatniks?

Fashion is perhaps the most striking aspect of the Beatnik movement at first glance. They generally wore black clothing with berets and had an overall sleek design. This spoke volumes for the values they held when you really dive into the Beat, or Beatnik movement.

It was in America that the Beat movement began, Jack Kerouac and Herbert Huncke together introduced the name and term 'Beat Generation' during the late 1940s. Beatniks started in a simple format as a literary subculture.

The name Beatnik was a term coined by Herb Caen of the San Francisco Chronicle on the 2nd of April in 1958.

Allen Ginsberg's 'Howl' from 1956, Jack Kerouac's 'On the Road' from 1957 and William S. Burroughs 'Naked Lunch' from 1959 are considered some of the best known book examples from the Beat Generation movement.

Allen Ginsberg denounced what he saw as the destructive forces of capitalism and conformity in the United States, with his book Howl. He formed a friendship with Jack Kerouac and William S. Burroughs, together these guys formed the basis of what is known as the Beat movement. They were incredibly well known throughout the 60s era, inspiring many to become involved in what they did. With what I will explain about this movement, I'm sure you'll see why.

The Beatnik's main objective was the focus on topics that rejected the mainstream culture and its ideals. Celebrating nonconformity and spontaneous creativity. In essence, the Beat movement gave rise to many of the younger generation to question and challenge the social norms, alongside people who also shared similar values. They collectively challenged this so called "American Dream" with many of its other questionable aspects.

There was an Anti materialistic belief that was being formed and held by the Beatnik movement, this was in a response to people being driven by consumerism. People weren't materialistic, they were anti materialistic. They felt that everyone bought something new, but they then threw those items away, in favour of more new items. Getting rid of items or goods was hardly a society that favoured owning material goods or was "materialistic" from the Beatnik viewpoint. They felt the drive of consumerism was pushing a disaster known as "landfill" from these items that would be thrown away.

As a side note: Consumer credit was introduced in the 1950s. Banks introduced their own universal bank cards that allowed consumers to charge goods and services onto one account then pay off the debt over time. But while credit cards allowed more people to buy more things, equality was an issue. Some women and those considered to be a racial minority (such as African Americans) didn't have access to these new ways of consumer credit.

After WW2, the production of goods encouraged an influx of jobs within the transport industry, the home appliance industry and so on. These new consumer products such as cars, TVs, heaters and fridges were at the top of the list for those looking at modernising their homes. This new 'consumer credit' became popular for people to afford new things.

Community: One big hub of activity was forming in San Francisco, being that it was a top tourist destination in the USA, it soon became a base and home for many of the Beat movement. The San Francisco Renaissance was formed and became a unit of poetic and literary activity. It has also been cited now that it also encompassed the visual and performing arts, philosophy, cross cultural interest and new social sensibilities. In short, it was a collection of educated visionaries.

The Civil Rights Act, the Women's liberation movement and the Anti war movement, among other movements, all branched out of this original literary Beat movement.

What about the British Beatniks? Aren't they being left behind?

Well, it's a bit of a sad story here really. The UK Beat movement didn't really happen in any notable fashion in the UK, most of what did happen was largely inspired by the American sub culture of the same name. Not a great wealth of information can be sourced regarding the UK Beat movement, this may largely be a result of the issues the Beatniks fought against themselves, the issues in the UK were far less apparent compared to the United States. This lack towards a need for action likely played a role in the thin quantity of UK Beatniks.

For the American youth, their issues were far more further reaching, whereas in the UK, the issues still remained, but socially the individuals in the UK were far more individualistic. In America, society as a whole was more creative. But even though this may appear to be the case, both sides were inclined to hang out in cafés, rather than in bars or pubs. They shared a generalized sense of resistance to 'The Establishment'. Likewise, both sides evolved and progressed into what we more commonly associate the 60s with... Hippies! But we have yet more UK youth cultures.

Mods and Rockers

Mods:

Mods in the UK, well, this could almost follow an evolution of the Ted youth culture. In essence, the Teddy Boys paved the way for making male interest in fashion socially acceptable. The name Mod was short hand for Modernists which means; Mods wore suits and other clean-cut outfits, along with hairstyles of a similar nature, they listened to music genres such as modern jazz, soul, Motown, SKA and British, blues-rooted bands like The Yardbirds, The Small Faces and The Who. Typically, the Mods are known to be the trendsetters of the time, so they were 'modern'.

The youth of the early 1960s was one of the first generations who didn't have to contribute their money from their after-school jobs to the family finances. This allowed the money to be spent on consumer products, music, fashion and of course, on the Italian scooters, such as the Lambretta's and Vespa's. These scooters were adorned with many mirrors, lamps, stickers and accessories of all kinds. The scooters were an artistic expression of what the Mod stood for.

The Mods could be noted as being a working class version of the middle class Beatniks, both used to hang out in cafés. The coffee bars were a hub of activity for the British youth culture, in contrast to the 'old traditional' pub goer. The Beatniks and early Mods were a stand alone youth culture, but shared similar values of going against the grain, forming new and up to date lifestyles, they both opposed mainstream society. Beatniks were not as rowdy, they weren't as brutish in comparison, and were more left wing in their political sense towards society. But they shared some basic traits at least. So, I'm not comparing them directly, it would be more of a generalisation.

The coffee bars or cafés were open until the early hours of the morning. Coffee bars had jukeboxes, in some cases they reserved a space in the machines for the customers' own records. As I mentioned earlier, the younger generation had more disposable income, so likely had records of their own. Although this was so, these records were highly valuable to the individual who owned them.

Until the mid 60s, there weren't any music festivals in the UK. A newly emerging music festival soon changed this in 1963 called 'The National Jazz and Blues Festival'. It was headed by jazzmen Chris Barber and Johnny Dankworth, then by 1965, the event leaned heavily towards rock music with bands like The Who, The Yardbirds, Manfred Mann and The Animals. The Mods flocked to this festival by the thousands in Richmond, which is a London Borough. An all in ticket cost £1. However, due to many complaints by the local residents, the event was moved to Windsor in 1966, then again to Reading after that. These Richmond festivals were the apex of the Mod sub culture though.

The band The Who created an album reflecting this Mod culture called Quadrophenia, released in 1973. A film of the same name was released in 1979. Both the album and film are based on the early to mid 60s era of the Mod sub culture. The film is depressing in some ways, pay attention to the beginning, it will make the ending make sense. It is now of course a cult classic.

In the late 60s the Mod culture began to evolve and change. This was due to the commodification of aspects the Mods stood for, a value to keep things modern or up to date, they changed. They eventually splintered off into other forms such as the 'Skinheads'.

Rockers:

We have the Rockers. The Rockers could be drawn in comparison to the earlier Teds, but with the added bonus of motorcycles. Both the Teds and Rockers followed Rock and Roll music. Rocker motorbikes were not just merely used as transport but were used as an object of intimidation and masculinity. If you understand modern internet slang, the 50s and 60s rocker was their version of our modern day Chad.

The bikes placed them uneasily close to death on various occasions. The bikes were stripped down and modified in an attempt to make them more like sports bikes. The 'Ton-up boys' were another term or alternate version of the Rocker. Cafés began popping up in support of these newly emerging youth cultures. ACE Café in London is a surviving example of the Rocker cafés, it is a shining example of the cafés that accommodated these youth cultures. Billy Fury and Johnny Kidd were pre Beatle inspirations for the Rockers, Rock and Roll music was their escape from normality. Elvis Presley was inspirational of course, that goes without saying. I will list a few songs at the end of the Mods and Rockers section that they would have listened to.

Because the aesthetic was based around intimidation, they were people who didn't take any sh!t and weren't scared of death. The many dancehalls and other events weren't keen or didn't have the ability to cater for the Rockers, or their other variants. So, they spent their time at the cafés that did.

The culture that began in the 1950s was commonly known as the Ton-up boys. A British slang term "Ton" meant "Doing a ton down the road" typically meaning going at 100mph (160kph). To do so was seen as an achievement of riding skills and mechanical modification skills. Like the Mods, the Ton-up boys and Rockers had additional disposable income due to the post war rise in prosperity and income rises. The recent availability of credit and financing for young people helped both the Mods and Rockers.

This is my own opinion here from my own family and my understanding towards the mods and rockers; the Rockers or Ton-up boys, to be precise, came through the post war era, many young people were not scared of death, having faced war first hand; the whole strong aesthetic coming largely because soldiers embodied just that.

Intimidating, fearless, strong and dependable. But when these young people returned to civilian life, the world looked and felt alien, far removed from the social aspects that warfare had to offer. So, these antics of riding dodgy motorcycles you modified in your back shed, and then riding them at 100mph became a 'good idea'!? Becoming part of a gang became attractive, these people had lost the fear of death anyway, so why not? This mind-set likely stayed as part of the overall aesthetic, especially for many who followed on from this first iteration of Motorcycle youth culture. The Hell's Angels are an example of this evolution.

Mods Vs Rockers

The Mods and Rockers had largely opposing views with one another. Their conflicts were heavily publicised, the mass media started targeting these socially powerless youths to cast them as "folk devils", creating in some cases a moral panic. But for the youth cultures themselves, this helped to provoke a stronger meaning behind who they were and who they could be. In other words, it did little to prevent them from happening or from becoming 'folk devils'. This publicity helped to change the name from Ton-up boys into Rockers. For the public opinion, which was helped through the media, they came to consider the Rockers as hopelessly naive, loutish, scruffy, motorcycle cowboys. They were the loners and or outsiders of society. (Where can I join?)

This image of a rebel without a cause was synonymous with James Dean, an American actor. A film in 1955 of the same name, "Rebel without a cause" was a clear depiction of the youth culture at the time and how people saw James Dean. One could say he was an icon for this reason. I cannot actually put a link between the Rockers and James Dean directly, but the influence and message the film likely had would have influenced the youth at the time. The rebel look was formed into a romantic image, a sex symbol of sorts, an intellectual and an outsider of society, but in a good way. (Again, where do I join, right?) James Dean certainly reflected this image during the 1950s.

Bosley Crowther, writing in The New York Times, described Rebel Without a Cause as;

"violent, brutal and disturbing", and as an excessively graphic depiction of teen-agers and their "weird ways".

The Mods and Rockers typically spent their time in the southeast coastal towns of England. The growing youth trends of Brighton and Hastings were a haven for these youth cultures. Arcades, lights, dance halls and the seaside were top attractions. Then in 1964, it's the May bank Holiday weekend, 4 stroke engines roar down the roads and 2 stroke scooters pop along the roads as well. A brawl and fight broke out that lasted for two days in Brighton. It was alleged the fight started due to a pebble being tossed at the feet of the Rockers by a Mod. Deck chairs were flying in the air, along with fists, angry words and pebbles of course.

Newspapers wrote about the seaside brawl as being out of "disastrous proportions", and labelled mods and rockers as "internal enemies". As this was in England, they said it would "bring about disintegration of a nation's character" and would "surge and flame like a forest fire", all rather British and dramatic.

The later film Quadrophenia depicted this seaside brawl scene. It was a highly iconic event, making both sides of the party legendary in their own right. The Mods and Rockers were like two tribes that went to war, yes, I know, calm down Holly Johnson...

American Mods and Rockers?

What about the Americans in all of this? Did they not have a youth culture that was much the same? Well, yes, in a way?

In a similar situation to the Beatniks, they weren't as prominent in the UK but they certainly were in America, it's the opposite way around with the Mods and Rockers, they were popular in the UK but not in America. The styles of clothing were a shared trait between America and the UK though. The Mods and Rockers weren't as strong in America, but in the UK, the Mods and Rockers were far more well defined, again similar to the Beatniks.

American musicians, in the wake of the "British Invasion", which is something I will elaborate upon later, adopted the look of mod clothes, longer hairstyles, and Beatle boots.

It was somewhat more the style that was adopted, rather than the lived in lifestyle of the Mods and or Rockers. One thing America did have was the Hells Angels though, this developed and has its own history. But no mods or rockers though, really.

The Mods and Rocker music:

Mods:
'Green Onions', Brooker T. And the M.G's – 1962
'There's A Ghost In My House', R Dean Taylor – 1973
'My Generation', The Who – 1965
'You Really Got Me', The Kinks – 1964
' Heart Full Of Soul', The Yardbirds – 1965
Rockers:
'The Hop', Danny &.the Juniors – 1959
'Runaway', Del Shannon – 1961
'Halfway To Paradise', Billy Fury – 1959
'Shakin' All Over', Johnny Kidd & The Pirates – 1960
'Ready Teddy', Elvis Presley – 1956
(These wonderful songs can be found in the Spotify playlist, the playlist title is the same as the book title.)

The British Invasion

This is a term used to explain the "Invasion" of British music bands coming over to the United States of America. But so too came along the styles of clothing and other aspects of British culture. Such bands like The Beatles are a shining example of this phenomenon. "Beatlemainia" was something that sparked huge interest in the cultures on both sides of the Atlantic Ocean, each side wanted to know more about the other.

Many other British bands such as The Rolling Stones, The Kinks, The Who and many more soon followed the Beatles.

"I Saw Her Standing There" – The Beatles – 1963

"Not Fade Away" – The Rolling Stones – 1964

"All Day And All Of The Night" – The Kinks – 1964

" The Kids Are Alright" – The Who – 1965

(These songs are again found on the Spotify playlist.)

This wasn't just a one way street though, outside of music, other aspects of British art became popular in the US during this period, it led the U.S. media to proclaim the United Kingdom as the centre of music and fashion. So, this helped to boom the fashion trends in the United Kingdom, and its economy. Both sides trading each other off with aspects of art, youth culture, fashion and more. Things have never been the same since.

The Hippie counterculture became a real blend of both sides to the Atlantic Ocean, by 1967, the counterculture really did begin to blend aspects of both sides more noticeably. But I must say this, in retrospect it might be easy to class all the youth cultures as following a similar pattern of change, revolution, liberation, love and acceptance. But the youth cultures at the time were far more fragmented, they weren't so seemingly interconnected. Of course, change seemed to be emerging on the horizon, but what kind of emerging change was, at that time, less than immediately obvious. Thus, it isn't right to say that the youth cultures all held hands with one another, they were more likely to throw pebbles at each other instead.

The love child or Hippie

How did the name "Hippie" come about? Terms like "Hips", "Hip" and "Hipster" became fashionable slang words during the 60s. This was because people were considered to be "in the know" or "cool", as opposed to being "Square", meaning to be conventional and also impossibly old-fashioned. The word 'Hippie' would be similar to our modern term 'woke' in many ways. Beatniks were seen as being on the right beat, or with what's going on. So, they were the ones to aim for and become.

Certain slang terms became hugely popular, phrases such as "To Dig" were terms of a more personal nature. Although 'to dig' was used to say, "I get you", "I understand you", or "I appreciate you", but 'to dig' had a better edge to it. It was almost a term that may suggest whilst someone may appreciate you, or understand you, they may also know that they, on the sly, may smoke some pot or weed. It became a term of phrase for those who 'knew' about something that others didn't.

"Groovy", well now, this might be an obvious choice when referencing 60s slang terms, but here we are. What can I say, it was incredibly popular at the time. The word groovy was very versatile in it's use; it covered a wide variety of 'things'. Mostly though, it was used to describe something that is either excellent or exciting. "That is some groovy music"

"Far out" was another term of phrase. While this didn't generally entertain drug use or pertain to the idea of doing so. The term usually meant either excellent, or was a similar par to "groovy" or, it could also be used to describe something unconventional and a little out of the norm. "That record is far out". It also likely had references to the technology of the time, or links towards the space age, far out in a way to mean 'not of this world'.

Early in the 60s the Beatniks started to use the term 'Hip'. A mixture of people soon changed the term into 'Hippie' and adopted the language and counter-cultural values of the Beat Generation. Because this happened as a phase transition from one into the other, it isn't possible to draw a definitive line between the Beatniks and the Hippies. The term Beatnik was still used throughout the 60s era, yet some people identified more with the name Hippie or love child rather than Beatnik. Beatniks and Hippies alike both advocated for social change and both shared similar values in one way or another. Beatniks were generally less politically minded to start with, whilst Hippies were certainly political in their views and aims for social change. Hippies created their own communities of varying size known as "Communes". They listened to psychedelic music, embraced the sexual revolution, especially with the arrival of the contraceptive pill, whilst many others used drugs such as marijuana or LSD to explore altered states of consciousness. Spirituality became very popular during the 60s era. Many aspects of art, pop culture and alternative music became expressive (hurrah LSD).

Such things like the VW campervan became an icon and symbol towards the rising Hippie subculture. The VW beetle, the campervan, Split screen, Bay window or many other names that these VW's go by, they generally became synonymous with the counterculture. There were other variants like the Karmann Ghia that became hugely popular. The simplistic design of the engine, it's ease of repair and maintenance, usability, economy and much more, they were huge selling points. All of these were aspects that fit neatly with the Hippie ethos of saving money, DIY and saving the environment, especially with their economy at the time. Some even chose to live in these campervans over living a 'conventional' lifestyle. They would use them to travel the country, escape the world and follow rock bands. The most notable rock band followers were the "Deadheads" who followed the American band The Grateful Dead. Some Hippies used these vehicles as statements, typically adorning them with flowers, artwork and accessories. Similar in a way to Mods who used their vehicles as statements. Because of this, many people today associate them as "THE Hippie Van". Nobody who thinks of a Hippie van thinks of a Honda. There is something nostalgic, romantic and rather understandable in these old cars, one can see almost an aspect of humanity within them. Disney knew this and made the famous Herbie franchise out of it. Today, they fetch a lot of money because of this, some reaching staggering amounts for what they are actually worth. It would be the icon that people pay for, clearly not the mechanical or technological aspects... obviously!?

I personally love the Early Bay window campervan myself, or the later Split screen campervan. But everyone likes certain models, trim choices, original factory options and so forth. Today they are as popular as they ever were. Perhaps you prefer other old classic cars? What would you own?

One of the most admirable traits of the Hippie movement was an embrace of support for the socially deprived, or the down trodden of society. Many people started advocating for radical changes to occur, all in the light of being this 'new era of humanity'. "Make love not war", "Hell No – Don't go" these slogans were very much associated with anti war protests. And protest they did!

Hippies were a collection of loving people, keen on change for the better. The media portrayed these Hippie subcultures poorly and cynically, most likely because any deep and expansive change is often feared.

The Hippie sub culture was all about protests, marches, following bands, colourful clothing styles and all the rest, very much counter-culture. But it was more than just a style! It was a serious thing; it was a lifestyle in and of itself. It was a lifestyle that was incredibly flexible, people could bring up their children in many alternative ways, they chose love itself as a guiding force. They had spirituality as a foundation to work their ethics from, Zen Buddhism became very popular during the 60s. The environment, recycling, love for nature and concern for others are all aspects of the hippie sub-cultures.

All in all, the Hippie movement was very unique for it's time, we haven't seen anything like it since the 60s, but why that is I will explore in the later chapters of this book. The Hippie itself was a formation of many cultural changes that were occurring outside of the 60s, and further back in time. I hope to have pointed this out within the Beatnik section of this chapter, in a way, the hippie was an inevitability.

Christian the Lion

After talking about the Hippies and the counterculture, the youth of the 60s may be understood as encompassing a loving embrace between one human and another. Well, this story certainly squashes that.

Picture this, it's 1969, we're in London, the capital of the UK. Harrods, which is an upmarket department store, they have just bought a lion cub from a zoo in Ilfracombe, Devon, which had gone bankrupt. A typical day of course in the UK.

Two men called John Rendall and Anthony "Ace" Bourke then purchase the lion cub, you know, as you do on a weekend. The two men brought him back to their London home. The lion cub was called Christian, but as he got larger, the men moved Christian to their furniture store, ironically named Sophistocat.

This situation worked well for the local media, they were keen to picture the lion and the two men. People came to the store just to see if the two men actually had a real lion, and not just a stuffed animal of some kind instead.

Rendall and Bourke obtained permission from a local minister to exercise Christian at the Moravian church graveyard just off from King's Road and Milman's Street, Chelsea. The men also took the lion to local restaurants feeding him steaks, as a humble ham sandwich wasn't up to par at this point.

It became a difficult time though as the two men soon realised, they couldn't keep Christian the Lion forever. This was due to his growing size and increasing costs of care. It became a top priority to provide Christian with the home that he needed, and with the love they had for him. Calling upon their friends Bill Travers and Virginia McKenna, stars of the film 'Born Free', they visited Rendall and Bourke's furniture store and met Christian. They suggested that Bourke and Rendall ask the assistance of George Adamson. Mr Adamson was an advocate for lions in Kenya with his wife Joy, they agreed to reintegrate Christian into the wild at their compound in the Kora National Reserve, Kenya.

Virginia McKenna wrote about the experience in her memoir 'The Life in My Years', published March 2009.

After Christian was successfully integrated into the Kora National Reserve, Kenya, Rendall and Bourke went to visit him in 1972. They travelled to Kenya to visit Christian and were filmed in a UK documentary 'Christian, The Lion at World's End' (released in the U.S. as Christian the Lion). The video can be watched on YouTube today. (Go and watch it, you know you want to). The two men were advised by the people at the Reserve that Christian may not remember them, and cautiously stood by as Christian came strolling along to meet them. Christian quickly leaped up playfully onto the two men, standing on his hind legs and wrapping his front legs around their shoulders. A warm embrace of lost old friends. Christian also introduced some friends he had made whilst living at the Reserve, two lionesses, Mona and Lisa. He also introduced them to a foster cub named Supercub.

This is a romantic story of love, courage and animal welfare. It also strikes as a difference between the British and American cultures as well. Whilst the American culture was at this time socially expressive, alternative and unique. The British culture on the other hand were different in contrast, the people themselves were more eccentric, unique and individualistic. Such aspects like fashion were a clear contrast between the two, but the sub cultures were also unique to each side of the Atlantic Ocean.

But one shared value that was held by both sides of the Atlantic Ocean was the women's liberation, or perhaps lack thereof.

Women's Liberation Movement

The Women's Liberation Movement, or the women's Lib for short, was actually the 2nd wave of feminism that occurred during the 60s. The 1st wave occurred roughly during the 1840s, it emerged from an environment of urban industrialism and liberal, socialist politics. Elizabeth Cady Stanton (d.1902) drafted the 'Seneca Falls Declaration', which outlined the new movement's ideology and political strategies.

The 2nd wave is when things really began to change and alter, but the 'radical' changes were happening when many other aspects of society were also changing.

Despite the many positive socioeconomic transformations occurring at the time, our cultural attitudes, especially concerning work and our legal system, they all combined forces to reinforce gender inequalities during the 60s. Due to these many gender inequalities at the time, a liberation movement unsurprisingly began to arise, the Women's Liberation Movement was born, or at least took off in a serious way.

There wasn't a single way, movement nor approach that actually aimed to deal with these issues collectively, or perhaps better to say worked cohesively within the Women's Liberation. This was mainly because many aspects spanned various cultural avenues, so cohesion between women collectively was difficult. But while this was in some ways a bad thing, what was good is they wanted women whose voices had been silenced to come forwards, they then wanted them to become able to express their own views and solutions. These women who brought about these changes were known as feminists. Some feminists rose a sub movement known as "consciousness-rising" where sessions were aimed at politicizing personal issues. Other movements focused on changing societal perception rather than reforming legislation. At times this led to rivalry between women of the liberation. So, again there wasn't much cohesion in some areas. The philosophy practiced by these liberationists amassed a global sisterhood of support, all working to eliminate inequality. All women felt that they experienced a second class narrative that weaved into employment, family and society. Well, they weren't wrong!

The women's liberation movement sadly only began in the UK during the later half of the 60s. Again, the UK lags behind America, all I can say is we only have tiny legs, I guess?

We are in the UK, it's 1972, a new magazine tries to re-shape women's literature. This was the Cosmopolitan magazine, Helen Gurley Brown, the author created a magazine version of her own life. She was visiting places never visited before with her magazine.

The Cosmopolitan spoke about sex as a topic, opening up conversations that may never would have happened prior. In the 1960s, Helen Brown was an outspoken advocate of women's sexual freedom and sought to provide women with role models throughout her magazine. Betty Friedan, author of 'The Feminine Mystique', she disliked what Brown was doing with the magazine. Friedan's reception followed that Brown was creating an "anti-feminist" and an "immature teenage-level sexual fantasy". For this reason, it wouldn't be untrue to say views towards the Cosmopolitan magazine were mixed at the time.

The Women's England football team is another aspect. It was ground-breaking, beginning in the early 70s. I will say it was awful, not the team though, but the reception women received at the time! This poor reception was coming from both presenters and sexist fans, it's fair to say the sport was certainly patronised. But it opened the doors for women to become a part of a previously male dominated platform. So, women were beginning to become part of human society as if women were humans, who knew!?

A few stand out notable feminists of the 60s & 70s were Gloria Steinman, Angela Davis, Betty Friedan, Juliet Mitchell, Sheila Rowbotham and Sally Alexander.

British feminists:

Juliet Mitchell was a prominent British feminist. Mitchell's notable article "Women: The Longest Revolution", in the 'New Left Review' during 1966, was an original synthesis made from inspirations via Simone de Beauvoir, Frederich Engels, Viola Klein, Betty Friedan and other analysts of women's oppression. Mitchell also founded the 'Centre for Gender Studies' at Cambridge University. She is also noted for her book "Psychoanalysis and Feminism: Freud, Reich, Laing and Women", published in 1974. The book tried to reconcile psychoanalysis and feminism at a time when many considered them as incompatible. This book is an essential to the feminist Canon.

Sheila Rowbotham was another British feminist and literary historian; she published a pamphlet in 1969 called "Women's Liberation and the new politics". The pamphlet cited that Socialist theory needed to consider the oppression of women in cultural and economic terms. She examined the experiences of women involved in radical and revolutionary movements in Cuba, Algeria, Vietnam, China, Russia, France and Britain from the 17th century up to the 20th century. Sheila cited that only through these radical movements have any changes been made. Her findings were published in two books: "Women, Resistance and Revolution" released in 1972, and "Hidden from History" released the following year in 1973. Wonderful books! Again, essential to the feminists Canon.

Sally Alexander was also a British feminist. She was a leading organiser of the 1970 'Miss World Protests'. Alexander was portrayed by Keira Knightley in the 2020 British comedy-drama "Misbehaviour" about her involvement in the 1970 Miss World competition. You can likely watch it on one of our many platforms today, it would serve as a more visual tool rather than a literary one, as so far, I've only shared book ideas.

American feminists:

Gloria Steinem is undoubtedly recognised as an American leader for the Women's Liberation Movement.

Steinem: "A feminist is anyone who recognises the equality and full humanity of women and men".

This quote and others she had really struck a deep chord with the women of American society. Her efforts went far deeper than supportive quotes though. Steinem was both the co-founder to a magazine called "Ms." and a journalist for the New York magazine. She gained national attention in 1969 with her article called "After Black Power, Women's Liberation." This cemented her as a leader of the Women's

Liberation Movement. She wasn't just a writer any longer, Steinem helped found the National Women's Political Caucus (NWPC) during 1971 with 300 other women. She gave a speech on the day of founding the NWPC, which is considered to be one of the greatest speeches of the 20th century! Not only did the speech address the issues of sexism and misogyny, but also to those of racism and social class. Steinem refers to the idea of sex and race as being easy ways to organize people into inferior and superior beings. This is due to the prominent characteristics and traits that are easy to point out, along with the class system that does this also, or sees both men and women as its own class system, strong and weak.

Steinem went on to do great work for the Women's Liberation Movement, she has continued throughout the ensuing decades up to this day! A truly fabulous woman.

Angela Davis is an American Marxist, feminist political activist, philosopher, academic and author. She was a force of liberation supporting Black women of America during the 60s and 70s. Davis wasn't just involved in the Women's Lib but was also fighting for the Civil Rights Movements as well. She believed racism and capitalism were absolute dangers to American justice, they still are in all honesty.

In 1969, Angela became a professor of philosophy at the University of California at Los Angeles. The governor of California at the time, Ronald Reagan, learned about Angela's political connections and pressured the university to fire her! She managed to take the case to court, and she won the case, which is a victory in and of itself! But disaster struck when the University fired her over concerns about her political views claiming that her "Speeches were too politically provocative". Yes, really!

She lived an amazing life, full of hardships, wonder and success! She felt that women had a difficult time in society, reflecting the same in her views towards racism. She had this to say:

"Racism is deeply embedded in the very fabric of this country — it's economy, it's political structures, and all the institutions which form the basis of this society."

Betty Friedan

"In almost every professional field, in business and in the arts and sciences, women are still treated as second-class citizens. It would be a great service to tell girls who plan to work in society to expect this subtle, uncomfortable discrimination--tell them not to be quiet, and hope it will go away, but fight it. A girl should not expect special privileges because of her sex, but neither should she "adjust" to prejudice and discrimination."

Friedan was of course a feminist and prominent author. Her 1963 book "The Feminine Mystique" is often credited as sparking the second wave of American feminism altogether, quite a remarkable book and author!

The female restrictions of the 50s, the trapped and imprisoned feelings of oppression felt by women, along with those who were forced into these stereotypical roles, they all rightfully needed a change! Her book spoke deeply for American women who soon began attending 'consciousness-raising' sessions and lobbying for the reform of oppressive laws and social views that restricted females. This aspect certainly stands proudly amongst the political aspects of feminism.

By 1966, Friedan co-founded and became the first president of the National Organization for Women (NOW). Friedan was inspired by the failure of the "Equal Employment Opportunity Commission" to enforce "Title VII" of the "Civil Rights Act of 1964", but with other founders, they collected in Friedan's hotel room and put together the NOW organisation. NOW lobbied to enforce the Title VII of the Civil Rights Act of 1964, and the Equal Pay Act of 1963, and, they managed to win the fight, the first two major legislative victories of the movement! Huge victories for women's oppression.

In 1971 Friedan, along with many other leading the women's lib, including Gloria Steinem (with whom she had a legendary rivalry) founded the National Women's Political Caucus (NWPC).

Friedan as well as others have reshaped the Women's Liberation Movement, feminists have tirelessly campaigned for access to contraception, abortion, and all forms of reproductive healthcare, empowering women with freedom, choice and autonomy over their bodies and lives ever since the 60s! Without these women and what happened during the 60s, we wouldn't have what we call today, feminism.

In retrospect of the mid 20th century Women's Liberation Movement, feminism had its foundations in equality as the main selling point. Spirituality was also a hot topic during this era as well, so names like 'consciousness rising' seemed more acceptable. The 60s Women's Liberation Movement really was a blend of all things for the people, by the people and in liberation for people overall.

Some songs here reflect the 60s and 70s women's liberation movement,

"You Don't Own Me" – Lesley Gore – 1963 this song truly highlighted women's empowerment during this early 60s era. It was one of the first feminist Anthems of its kind, in Lesley Gores own words: "I just can't find anything stronger to be honest with you, it's a song that just grows every time you do it."

"The Pill" – Loretta Lynn – 1972/75? (Made in 72 but was cancelled due to the wording thus released in 75). This song is rather controversial, but it highlights the freedom women get from the contraceptive pill.

"I Am Woman" – Helen Reddy – 1971 (This was and possibly still is an Anthem of the women's liberation movement, it certainly was during the 70s after the apex of the counter-culture movement.)

"Sisters, O Sisters" – Yoko Ono – 1972. This was originally written by Yoko Ono, it first appeared on John Lennon's and Yoko Ono's 1972 Plastic Ono Band album 'Some Time in New York City', backed by Elephant's Memory.

(These songs are on the music playlist on Spotify.)

Summary:
Overall, this is a brief introduction to the many aspects of the 1960s. The 60s goes much further, much deeper than one chapter can accommodate. I will begin this deep dive by presenting the second chapter...

Chapter 2

The Civil Rights Movement

Because the Civil Rights Movement of the 60s was so vast and intrinsic to the 60s, I feel it requires a whole chapter of its own. Thus, I want to give the right space for such an important aspect of humanity.

By the end of the 50s and moving into the 60s, as soon as 1961, a book of non fiction was published by the writer and journalist John Howard Griffin. The book was called 'Black like me' which recounts his own journey through the southern States of America. He temporarily darkened his skin to pass as a black man. He travelled for 6 weeks documenting himself and his findings as a life lived on the other side of the colour line. John travelled through Alabama, Arkansas, Louisiana, Mississippi and Georgia. By 1964 a film version of the book was produced. Griffin became a celebrity for a short while because of this. But essentially, this book and film brought to the attention for many white Americans the true horrors of real life experiences, especially for a country which supposedly supported equality, but in fact actually didn't. Racial discrimination was acknowledged by a large number of white Americans, but not by all though. Americans at the time associated racism with the horrendous anti Semitism of Nazi Germany.

This book may have had an impact for the need to evaluate the civil rights for many American people. The Civil Rights Act was introduced in 1964, the act explicitly banned all racial discrimination, including racial segregation in schools, public accommodation and businesses. But because a large majority of American states work independently, a large change needed to occur.

The same can be said for the United Kingdom, the law at the time was not in favour of, nor did it support Afro-Caribbean citizens. Many pubs had notices outside stating "No Blacks, No Irish and No Dogs", this was OK by law at the time.

I will list a series of events that occurred in America and the UK to outline the changes that were made during the 60s. But to do so, I have to start with the 1950s era.

1955, The Montgomery Bus Boycott, America.

Considered by some to be the mother of the modern day civil rights movement, we have the wonderful Rosa Parks. The story begins during December of 1955, segregation laws at the time stated that Black passengers on the bus system must sit in designated seats at the back of the bus. So, in short, the public bus network in Montgomery, and America by and large had a racially discriminative set up for passengers. A white male was unable to sit down, Rosa Parks quite rightfully refused to give up her seat, this caused her to be arrested.

What an outrage this caused! Soon after this, led by Baptist minister Martin Luther King Jr. and others, they formed the Montgomery Improvement Association (MIA). The MIA formed The Montgomery Bus Boycott, which lasted a whooping 381 days! Finally, on November 14, 1956, the Supreme Court ruled segregated seating was immoral. This marked one of the first changes to law held by and conducted via those discriminated by the law itself.

This event placed Martin Luther King Jr. front and centre in the fight for civil rights. He has remained the figurehead of the Civil Rights

Movements ever since. Gaining a considerably positive attitude for himself and others.

A saddening story goes for Rosa Parks though, in the wake of the Montgomery Bus Boycott, Parks consequently lost her tailoring job, whilst receiving death threats from white Americans. She and her family had to move to Detroit, Michigan in 1957 because of this. However, a touch of positivity, she remained an active member of the NAACP (National Association for the Advancement of Coloured People). She worked for the Congressman John Conyers from 1965-1988 helping homeless people find housing. She is an all round wonderful woman.

1958, Notting Hill Race Riots, United Kingdom.

We are in the UK, it's 1958 now following World War 2, the economy was struggling. In 1948 though, the British Nationality Act gave Citizenship of the UK to all people living in the British Empire. The British government began to encourage mass immigration from this point onwards to help fill shortages in the labour market. Many immigrants were attracted by advertisements towards much better prospects in what was often referred to as "The Mother Country".

Remember the Teddy Boys from the first chapter? Oh dear! Hideously racist Teddy boys were beginning to display hostility towards black families in the Notting Hill area, a situation exploited and inflamed by groups such as "Oswald Mosley's Union Movement" and other far-right groups such as the "White Defence League", they had an unashamed motto of "Keep Britain White".

The Notting Hill Race Riots are speculated to have begun with a lady called Majbritt Morrison, a white Swedish woman. On the 29th of August in 1958, Morrison and her Jamaican husband Raymond were in an argument near a local underground train station. Various white youths attempted to become involved in the situation, some got into a fight with Raymond and his friends. The following day Mrs Morrison was physically and verbally attacked by the same youths, some reports state different accounts of what happened. One report says she was attacked with an iron bar, other reports say she had racial slurs thrown at her along with milk bottles. The evening that followed this, a mob of up to 400 white youths and other people gathered around Bramley Road, they started attacking the houses of West Indian residents. The disturbances, rioting and attacks continued every night until the 5th of September.

The Metropolitan Police Commissioner stated that out of the 108 people, many were charged with crimes such as grievous bodily harm, affray and rioting and possessing offensive weapons. 72 were white and 36 were black. These riots caused tensions between the Metropolitan Police and the British African-Caribbean community. They claimed that the police had not taken their reports of racial attacks seriously enough, and I agree! Individual police officers said that there was racial motivation behind the disturbance, despite others saying there wasn't.

Activist Claudia Jones organized a 'Caribbean Carnival' in response to the riots, and also towards the state of race relations in Britain at the time. It was held on the 30th of January 1959 in St Pancras Town Hall. This was a precursor of the Notting Hill Carnival, which was first held during 1966, encapsulating the whole of Notting Hill, London. The Carnival still exists today, it is claimed to be the 2nd largest street Carnival in the world, attracting nearly three million people. I have been to the Carnival myself, and I must say it is an experience, wow!

1961, The Albany Movement, America.

This was an attempt at desegregation and a push for voters' rights coalition formed in Albany, Georgia, during November of 1961. The movement was helped by members of the "Student Nonviolent Coordinating Committee" (SNCC), and the "National Association for the Advancement of Coloured People" (NAACP). These groups were assisted by Martin Luther King Jr. and the Southern Christian Leadership Conference (SCLC).

Many claim the movement was a flop, really, but others disagree. They claim it as a beneficial lesson in strategy and tactics for the leaders of the Civil Rights Movement. Martin Luther King Jr. who was involved had this to say on the movement:

"The mistake I made there was to protest against segregation generally rather than against a single and distinct facet of it. Our protest was so vague that we got nothing, and the people were left very depressed and in despair. It would have been much better to have concentrated upon integrating the buses or the lunch counters. One victory of this kind would have been symbolic, would have galvanized support and boosted morale.... When we planned our strategy for Birmingham months later, we spent many hours assessing Albany and trying to learn from its errors. Our appraisals not only helped to make our subsequent tactics more effective but revealed that Albany was far from an unqualified failure".

1963, The Bristol Bus Boycott, United Kingdom.

We are now in the early 60s, we have issues with public bus services again, but one in Bristol, UK! The Bristol Omnibus Company wouldn't employ Black or Asian people. Unsurprisingly, this was unethical and people spoke out against this injustice! An organisation called "The Bristol Bus Boycott" fought for the rights of Black and Asian citizens. It was founded by Roy Hackett and led by youth worker Paul Stephenson as the spokesperson of the group, it included Owen Henry, Audley Evans, Prince Brown and Guy Bailey.

It was a success! Securing employment of first non-white conductor, on the 17th of September 1963. It is now cited that this Boycott actually helped pass the later Race Relations Act, 1965, which made "racial discrimination unlawful in public places." This was followed by the Race Relations Act 1968, which extended the provisions to housing and employment.

In the 2009 New Year Honours, Stephenson was appointed an Officer of the Order of the British Empire (OBE), for his part in organising the bus boycott ("For services to Equal Opportunities and to Community Relations in Bristol.") Bailey and Hackett were also awarded OBEs!

1963, Birmingham Campaign, America.

Back to America, the goal of the Birmingham campaign was to end discriminatory economic policies in the Alabama city against African American residents. The campaign included a boycott of certain businesses that hired only white people or maintained segregated restrooms. The aim was that of peaceful protests, and to fill the local jails with as many people as possible, so as to cause unrest. Led by Martin Luther King Jr., James Bevel, Fred Shuttlesworth and others, the campaign of nonviolent direct action attracted widely publicized confrontations between young black students and white civic authorities. It was also organised by the Southern Christian Leadership Conference (SCLC). Local authorities such as the fire department used high pressure water hoses against these peaceful protestors. The media coverage managed to help gain global support for these protestors.

Was it a success? It positively flourished King's reputation, ousted American politician Bull Connor from his office, forced desegregation in Birmingham, and directly paved the way for the Civil Rights Act of 1964. So, absolutely!

It convinced President Kennedy to address the severe inequalities between black and white citizens in the South:

"The events in Birmingham and elsewhere have so increased cries for equality that no city or state or legislative body can prudently choose to ignore them."

1963, March on Washington, America.

This event is known by 3 names: The March on Washington for Jobs and Freedom, The March on Washington or The Great March on Washington. This is perhaps the most iconic moment for the Civil Rights Movement of the 60s. Martin Luther King Jr. gave his famous speech "I have a dream". The march was to advocate for the civil and economic rights of African Americans. Nearly 250,000 people marched, including 60,000 white participants. It was heavily publicised at the time, with an incredible amount of pre planning ahead of the march itself. This pre planning was likely inspired by these previous events.

Because of the publicity the march attracted, many celebrities came to join the protests. Joan Baez led the crowds in several verses of "We Shall Overcome" and "Oh Freedom". Musician Bob Dylan performed "When the Ship Comes In", for which he was joined by Baez. Dylan also performed "Only a Pawn in Their Game", a provocative song, it wasn't a popular choice because it asserted that Byron De La Beckwith, as a poor white man, was not personally nor primarily to blame for the murder of Medgar Evers. Beckwith was a member of the Ku Klux Klan from Greenwood, Mississippi, he murdered the civil rights leader Medgar Evers on June 12, 1963. This was only 2 months prior to the March on Washington, so was very raw at the time. Bob Dylan must have had balls of steel at the time.

It is incredible to say in retrospect how important the publicity was for the music and protestors. The anti protest songs were something new, exciting and challenged "the Establishment". Many anti war protest songs ensued after the early 60s and on into the early 70s. Martin Luther King Jr. saw the power of music with his protests combined in the mix.

The March on Washington further helped to pass the Civil Rights Act of 1964.

Martin Luther King Jr. 'I have a dream' speech spoke out against the American Dream, something I mentioned the Beatniks were against. It advocated for radical change in support of the racially oppressed in society. This likely made it easier to cross over these seemingly two separate sub cultures.

Martin Luther King Jr:

"I have a dream that one day on the red hills of Georgia sons of former slaves and the sons of former Slave-owners will be able to sit down together at the table of brotherhood. I have a dream that one day even the state of Mississippi, a state sweltering with the heat of injustice, sweltering with the heat of oppression, will be transformed into an oasis of freedom and justice. I have a dream that my four little children will one day live in a nation where they will not be judged by the colour of their skin but by the content of their character. I have a dream . . . I have a dream that one day in Alabama, with it's vicious racists, with its governor having his lips dripping with the words of Interposition and nullification, one day right there in Alabama little black boys and black girls will be able to join hands with little white boys and white girls as sisters and brothers."

"We Shall Overcome" – Joan Baez – 1963 (Many versions of this song were made, but this particular event made this song an anthem during the civil rights movement).

"Oh Freedom" – Joan Baez – 1963 (This song was originally recorded by Odetta in 1956 as part of the "Spiritual trilogy", this was on her album titled "Odetta sings ballads and blues").

"When The Ship Comes In" – Bob Dylan & Joan Baez – 1963 (This particular song was recorded at the March on Washington, 1963).

"Only A Pawn In Their Game" – Bob Dylan – 1963 (It was released on his album 'The Times They Are A-Changin' 1964. Again, it is a controversial song!)

(All of these songs are on the Spotify playlist.)

The Civil Rights Movement

1964, Paul Stephenson, United Kingdom.

Paul Stephenson was back on the media radar again in 1964. He claimed national attention and fame for refusing to leave a local pub in Bristol, after ordering a half pint of beer. He refused to leave a public house called "The Bay Horse Pub" until he was served, resulting in a trial and charge of failing to leave a licensed premises.

At the time in the UK, it wasn't unusual to see signs on pubs stating, "No Blacks, no Irish and no dogs", being legally discriminative but also socially acceptable. His campaigns paved the way for the first Race Relations Act, in 1965 the following year. Following this, Stephenson left Bristol to work in Coventry as a Senior Community Relations Officer. In 1972 he went to London to work for the Commission for Racial Equality. Not only this, but while in London he worked with boxer Muhammad Ali setting up the "Muhammad Ali Sports Development Association" in Brixton.

To say Stephenson made a real change in the UK is an understatement, he helped many to gain a voice for speaking out against Racial discrimination.

1965, Bloody Sunday, America.

Bloody Sunday, also known as "The Selma to Montgomery marches" were three protest marches, held in 1965, along the 54-mile (87 km) highway from Selma, Alabama, to the state capital of Montgomery.

Prior to the first march, state officials in Selma, Alabama had turned off all of the nearby street lights, state troopers rushed at the protesters, attacking them, hence it's reference as "Bloody Sunday". Jimmie Lee Jackson was shot dead in a café after fleeing the scene with his grandfather and his mother.

On February 28 after Jackson's death, emotions were running high. A meeting was held at Zion United Methodist Church in Marion.

The meeting called for a march from Selma to Montgomery to talk to Governor George Wallace directly. Because tensions were high, the marches were focused directly on a nonviolent approach, many wanted to take violence as the reaction otherwise. An estimated 525 to 600 civil rights marchers headed southeast out of Selma on U.S. Highway 80.

After the Bloody Sunday march, President Johnson issued an immediate statement:

"Deploring the brutality with which a number of Negro citizens of Alabama were treated".

He also promised to send a voting rights bill to Congress that week, although it took him until March 15.

After the 3 marches occurred, with much of the marches receiving media coverage, it had a powerful effect on Washington. President Lyndon Baines Johnson's televised speech before Congress was broadcast nationally. It was considered to be a watershed moment for the civil rights movement. He said:

"Even if we pass this bill, the battle will not be over. What happened in Selma is part of a far larger movement that reaches into every section and state of America. It is the effort of American Negroes to secure for themselves the full blessings of American life. Their cause must be our cause, too, because it is not just Negroes but really it is all of us who must overcome the crippling legacy of bigotry and injustice. And we shall overcome".

On March 15, 1965, Johnson presented a bill to a joint session of Congress. The bill was passed that summer and signed by Johnson as the Voting Rights Act on August 6, 1965.

To say the marches were a success is without question, but at a terrible cost. Many in the Civil Rights Movement cheered the speech and were emotionally moved after so long, and so hard a struggle. Change really did seem possible, what an emotional time for humanity!

1965, Chicago Freedom Movement, America.

Lasting for two years from 65 – 66, called the Chicago Freedom Movement, also known as the "Chicago open housing movement", it was led by Martin Luther King Jr., James Bevel and Al Raby. The movement lobbied specific demands covering a wide range of areas besides open housing, it included quality education, transportation, job access, income and employment, health, wealth generation, crime and the criminal justice system, community development, tenant's rights, and quality of life.

After the arrest of a 21-year-old black man for drunk driving, on August 11th, 1965, riots ignited in an area called Watts, a predominantly black section of Los Angeles at the time.

The violence that ensued lasted for five days and resulted in 34 deaths, 3,900 arrests, and the destruction of over 744 buildings and 200 businesses in a 20-square-mile area. The riots shocked the nation and raised an awareness to the struggles urban blacks faced from outside South of America.

Inspired by this Movement and the events of the situation, Martin Luther King Jr. in 1967 wrote a book "Where Do We Go from Here: Chaos or Community?"

Being largely credited with inspiring the 1968 Fair Housing Act, the movement was the most ambitious of its kind up until this point.

1967, Vietnam War Opposition, America.

The war in Vietnam saw many people in America from all walks of life take action. Muhammad Ali, the Student Nonviolent Coordinating Committee (SNCC), and Martin Luther King Jr. compared the anti-war movement with the civil rights movement. They denounced U.S. involvement in a series of speeches, rallies and demonstrations. King's first public speech against the war, called "Beyond Vietnam," was delivered during April 1967 in front of 3,000 people at Riverside Church, New York.

Many songs occurred during the 60s in opposition to the Vietnam war, yet many other songs could be considered as protest songs. I will also list many out of the ordinary songs that we just haven't had since this time period. The 60s allowed music to be very experimental, unusual and raw. I will list some of these songs I feel are worth writing about. All of these songs can be found on a playlist on Spotify, the name of this playlist is the same as the book title.

"All You Need Is Love" – The Beatles – 1967
"All Along The Watchtower" – Bob Dylan & Jimi Hendrix – 1967/1968
"Draft Morning" – The Byrds – 1968
"Eve Of Destruction" – Barry McGuire – 1965
"Fortunate Son" – Credence Clearwater Revival – 1969
"For What It's Worth" – Buffalo Springfield – 1966
"Gimme Shelter" – The Rolling Stones – 1969
"Goin' Up The County" – Canned Heat – 1969
"Give Peace A Chance" – John Lennon, Yoko Ono – 1969
"Green River" – Credence Clearwater Revival – 1969
"Handsome Johnny" – Richie Havens – 1966
"I Feel Like I'm Fixing To Die Rag" – Country Joe McDonald – 1965
"Imagine" – John Lennon – 1971
"I Should Be Proud" – Martha Reeves & The Vandellas – 1970
"Masters Of War" – Bob Dylan – 1963
"Ohio" – Crosby, Stills, Nash and Young – 1970
"People, Let's Stop The War" – Grand Funk Railroad – 1972
"Song For David" – Joan Baze – 1970
"The End" – The Doors – 1967
"The Times They Are A-Changin" – Bob Dylan – 1964
"The Unknown Soldier" – The Doors – 1968
"Vietnam" – Jimmy Cliff – 1969
"What's Going On" – Marvin Gaye – 1971
"Where Have All The Flowers Gone" – Peter, Paul and Mary – 1962

1968, Poor People's Campaign, America.

The Poor People's Campaign is almost a follow on from the 1965 Freedom Movement in Chicago. But this campaign was held in Washington D.C. The campaign would lead up to a Poor People's March on the country's capital. Martin Luther King Jr. and the Southern Christian Leadership Conference (SCLC) were excited about the prospect of this campaign following the victories of the civil rights legislation, including the Civil Rights Act of 1964 and the Voting Rights Act of 1965. The Poor People's Campaign was still being planned when Martin Luther King Jr. was assassinated in Memphis, Tennessee, in April 1968. Nevertheless, the Poor People's March took place on June 19, 1968, led by Ralph Abernathy.

The Poor People's March was much smaller than King and others had originally planned, with an estimated 50,000 demonstrators participating. The marchers walked from the Washington Monument to the Lincoln Memorial, where they listened to speeches by Vice President Hubert Humphrey, Democratic presidential candidate Eugene McCarthy who was now King's widow, Coretta Scott King and Abernathy.

The marches didn't gain the results they were aiming for, but with the loss of King, the response to his death, more than 100 American inner cities exploded in rioting, looting and violence. It paled the campaign into insignificance.

The man who would be named as Martin Luther King Jr assassin was James Earl Ray, he has since testified that he was not the man who shot King. On the night of the shooting, presidential candidate Robert F. Kennedy emphatically announced King's death to a mostly Black audience at an inner city campaign rally:

"For those of you who are Black and are tempted to be filled with hatred and distrust at the injustice of such an act, against all white people, I can only say that I feel in my own heart the same kind of feeling. I had a member of my family killed, but he was killed by a white man. But we have to make an effort in the United States, we have to make an effort to understand, to go beyond these rather difficult times".

On such a sad night, it was the first time since 1963 that Kennedy had spoken publicly about the assassination of his brother, John F. Kennedy.

As many of you may know, J.F Kennedy was shot dead as he rode in a motorcade in Dallas, Texas, on November 22, 1963. His accused killer was Lee Harvey Oswald, a former U.S. Marine.

From this point onwards the Civil Rights Movement has been shaped in many ways, the people of America, as well as King are shining examples of humanity. They who fought oppression, violence and inhumanity, in spite of the difficulties, they are the ones who will be remembered, not the oppressors.

1965 – 1982, The Black Panther Party, worldwide.

John. Edgar Hoover, the Director of the Federal Bureau of Investigation (FBI), described the party as:

"The greatest threat to the internal security of the country."

Despite the passage of the 1960s civil rights legislation, many African Americans living in cities throughout North America continued to suffer both economic and social inequalities. Dire poverty and seriously reduced public services characterized these urban areas. Many black residents were subject to poor living conditions, joblessness, chronic health problems, violence and limited means to change their circumstances. In the wake of the assassination of Malcolm X in 1965, Merritt Junior College students; Huey P. Newton and Bobby Seale founded the Black Panther Party for Self-Defence on October 15, 1966.

Malcom X: He was an African American leader and a prominent figure in the Nation of Islam. Malcom articulated concepts of race pride with Black nationalism during the early 60s. After his assassination, the widespread distribution of his life story: "The Autobiography of

Malcolm X" published in 1965, made him an idol, hero and inspiration, especially amongst Black youth at the time.

Newton and Seale became an organisation, or better than that, a force of nature! They wanted to originally patrol the streets for African Americans, as a purpose made outfit to protect African Americans who weren't really protected and defend them against police brutality. Throughout their time, and through the simple idea of being your own hero among local society, they managed to coalesce into many other chapters. These chapters spread to many other major American cities, including San Francisco, New York City, Chicago, Los Angeles, Seattle and Philadelphia. They also became active in many prisons and formed international chapters in the United Kingdom and Algeria.

The first woman to join the party was Joan Tarika Lewis, in 1967. The Black Panthers also published their own newspaper named "The Black Panther". During 1969, the Party newspaper officially instructed male Panthers to treat female Party members as equals, portraying women as: "Intelligent political revolutionaries", exemplified by members such as Angela Davis, Erika Huggins and Kathleen Cleaver.

The Black Panther Party was also involved in many local community projects as part of their organization. These projects included community outreach, like the free breakfast for children program, education and health programs. Huey Newton expressed his support for the Women's Liberation Movement and also the Gay liberation movement during 1970. He published a letter in his newspaper "The Black Panther" reading:

"A Letter from Huey to the Revolutionary Brothers and Sisters About the Women's Liberation and Gay Liberation Movements".

Newton seemingly acknowledged women and homosexuals as oppressed groups; he urged the Black Panthers to "unite with them in a revolutionary fashion". This was only a year after the Stonewall Riots. This hardly showcases the group as dangerous, or only in it for the violence.

Scholars have characterized the Black Panther Party as the most influential black power organization of the late 1960s. Many stating the party was more criminal than political, characterized by "Defiant posturing over substance". This is hardly the picture their past seems to paint. But I am not a scholar, I am just a writer, I can only speculate.

This wasn't it for the women of the Black Panther Party, in 1974, as Huey Newton prepared to go into exile in Cuba, he appointed Elaine Brown as the first Chairwoman of the Party. Brown increased the influence of women Panthers by placing them in more visible roles within the previously male-dominated organization. She also hired Betty Van Patter in 1974 as a book keeper. Sadly, Van Patter went missing on December 13, 1974, after a dispute with Brown over financial irregularities of some kind. There was insufficient evidence for police to charge anyone, but the Black Panther Party leadership was "Almost universally believed to be responsible". Since the 70s, FBI files investigating Van Patter were destroyed in 2009 for reasons the FBI has declined to provide. Huey Newton had allegedly confessed to a friend that he had ordered Van Patter's murder, saying that Van Patter had been tortured and raped before she was killed, just to make matters even more complicated.

Not so many years after this, the Black Panther Party ended in 1982. The exponential expansion of the Black Panthers put strain on the original leading members. The scores of FBI spies (backed by millions in government-funding) to infiltrate and undermine the work of the party also didn't help. It's a highly speculative subject about exactly what ended the Party, but their legacy lives on. The party made a 10 – point program to challenge racism and challenge a capitalist system to its core:

1. We want freedom. We want power to determine the destiny of our Black Community.
2. We want full employment for our people.
3. We want an end to the robbery by the capitalists of our black and oppressed communities.
4. We want decent housing, fit for shelter of human beings.

5. We want education for our people that exposes the true nature of this decadent American society. We want education that teaches us our true history and our role in the present day society.
6. We want all Black men to be exempt from military service.
7. We want an immediate end to POLICE BRUTALITY and MURDER of Black people.
8. We want freedom for all Black men held in federal, state, county and city prisons and jails.
9. We want all Black people when brought to trial to be tried in court by a jury of their peer group or people from their Black Communities, as defined by the Constitution of the United States.
10. We want land, bread, housing, education, clothing, justice and peace.

So, in summary; The Civil Rights Movement during the 60s was a time of radical change, evoking multifaceted ranges of love, hate, crime, revolution and evolution. It spoke to pop culture, art, music and so much more. The fight against racism is still a prominent aspect of our society today, even though we aren't where we were during the 50s or 60s.

Racially oppressed citizens wasn't the only form of Liberation, the Gay Liberation was part of this mix towards helping and supporting the oppressed. This is certainly something that cannot be missed.

Chapter 3

PRIDE

The Gay Liberation Movement

To counter societal shame with gay pride is something we still share with our society today, it was no less the case during our 60s Western world either.

Many will say the "Stonewall riots" at the Stonewall Inn in Greenwich Village, Manhattan, New York City, was where it all began in June 1969. But this isn't entirely correct, the 1960s was a time of social upheaval in the West, the sexual revolution and counterculture influenced changes for the homosexual subculture as well. Many riots and protests came before Stonewall, but the difference here was that many people of the homosexual subculture became able to express the need for change publicly after Stonewall.

Some people may be unaware of Vanguard, which was a gay rights youth organization active from 1965 until 1967 in San Francisco. Adrian Ravarour, a priest led Vanguard for ten months and taught gay rights, then led Vanguard members in early demonstrations for equal rights. Glide Church began to sponsor Vanguard in June of 1966 assisting it to apply and become a non-profit organisation. However, the organization dissolved due to internal clashes in late 66 and early 67.

After the events of Stonewall, many People took to activism supporting homosexuality. Many people within the emerging gay liberation movement in the U.S. saw themselves as connected with the "New Left". Martha Shelley along with 20 or more men and women set up the "Gay Liberation Front" (GLF). The words "Gay Liberation" echoed "Women's Liberation". Yet the war in Vietnam had such an influence on the youth cultures during the 60s, the Gay Liberation Front consciously took its name from the National Liberation Fronts of Vietnam and Algeria also. These newly emerging social possibilities, including new social movements like Black Power, women's liberation and the student revolts, they all broke through a new era of radicalism. The newly forming GLF wanted to be part of that change.

For some, this unity was not desirable, and the "Gay Activists Alliance" (GAA) formed as a splinter group from GLF, they sought to focus more exclusively on gay rights. Other groups such as Radicalesbians and Street Transvestites Action Revolutionaries (STAR) also formed.

Martha Shelley wrote many articles for 'Come Out!', a New York City Gay Liberation Front newsletter. The newspaper's purpose was to be a voice for the GLF, this would promote LGBT rights, lesbian feminism and anti-sexism.

Her articles are listed below:
"Stepin' Fetchit Woman" (Vol. 1, No. 1)
"More Radical Than Thou" (Vol. 1, No. 2)
"The Young Lords" (Vol. 1, No. 3)
"Gay Youth Liberation" (Vol. 1, No. 4)
"Gays Riot Again! Remember Stonewall!" (Vol. 1, No. 5)
"Let a Hundred Flowers Bloom" (Vol. 1, No. 5) – Co-authored by Bernard Lewis
"Subversion in the Women's Movement: What is to be Done?" (Vol. 1, Issue 7)
"Power… and the People!" (Vol. 2, No. 7b)

Her political views and other commentary work towards gay liberation has been of remarkable inspiration towards many. She also allied with other groups like the Black Panther Party, Pro-choice Movement and Young Lords.

The Legalisation of Homosexuality

America:

The movement was doing well, during 1961, Illinois became the first state to squash its anti-sodomy laws, effectively decriminalizing homosexuality. A local TV station in California aired the first documentary about homosexuality, called "The Rejected", videos of this can be found on YouTube. (The Rejected, 1961).

In 2003, through "Lawrence v. Texas", all remaining laws against same-sex sexual activity were removed. In 2004, beginning in Massachusetts other states began to offer same-sex marriage, then in 2015, through "Obergefell v. Hodges", all states were required to offer same-sex marriage from then onwards.

Recent approval of same-sex marriage amongst 18-34 year olds, according to the General Social Survey, says support is near-universal. A 2022 Quinnipiac University poll found that 68 percent of Americans supported legal recognition of same-sex marriage and 22 percent opposed it.

United Kingdom:

In the United Kingdom, The Sexual Offences Act 1967 was passed. It decriminalised sex between two men over 21 but 'in private'. It did not extend to the Merchant Navy nor to the Armed Forces, or Scotland, Northern Ireland, the Channel Islands or the Isle of Man. Sex between two men remained illegal at this point in these cases.

The law was extended to Scotland by the Criminal Justice (Scotland) Act 1980, and to Northern Ireland by the Homosexual Offences (Northern Ireland) Order 1982.

In 1970 the London Gay Liberation Front (GLF) was established in the UK. It was based on the parallel movement in the US.

But in 1971 The Nullity of Marriage Act was passed, explicitly banning same-sex marriages between same-sex couples in England and

Wales. In 2013 however, the British Parliament passed the Marriage (Same Sex Couples) Act, which introduced civil marriage for same-sex couples in England and Wales. The legislation allowed religious organisations to opt in to marry same-sex couples should they wish to do so. But protected religious organisations and their representatives from successful legal challenge if they did not wish to marry same-sex couples. In Scotland, the Scottish Parliament has also legislated to allow same-sex marriages. The 'Northern Ireland Assembly' has not yet legislated to allow the marriage of same-sex couples in Northern Ireland at the time of printing this book.

Why things needed to change?

This may seem like a silly question, but the laws before these changes made homosexuality illegal. The British Parliament enacted the Criminal Law Amendment Act 1885, section 11, known as the 'Labouchere Amendment'. This prohibited gross indecency between males, regardless of what these men had achieved either for their country or for others socially.

To bring some context to this issue, let me bring to light a gentleman called Alan Mathison Turing (23 June 1912 – 7 June 1954).

He is considered by many to be the "Grandfather of Artificial intelligence". During WW2, he devised a number of techniques that assisted the breaking of German codes, including improvements to the pre-war Polish bomba method, an electromechanical machine that could find settings for the Enigma machine.

Alan played a vital role in enabling the Allies to defeat the Axis powers in many crucial engagements, including the 'Battle of the Atlantic'. He and his team are the true heroes of WW2. Their work is estimated to have shortened WW2 by two years and to have saved 14 million lives!

Because of his involvement and understanding of electronic technologies of the 1940s and coming 50s, he designed the "Automatic

Computing Engine", one of the first designs for a stored-program computer. He also came up with his "Turing Test" or known at the time as "The Imitation Game". This was a test of a machine's ability to exhibit intelligent behaviour equivalent to, or indistinguishable from, that of a human. Alan was speculative about Artificial intelligence during his lifetime, even though it wasn't as prominent as it is today. Many people today refer to his works on these matters.

Despite his achievements for both his country and society, he lived a double life. This is because of the British legal system. Turing was 39 when he started a relationship with Arnold Murray, who was unemployed at the time. Later, Alan's house was burgled, Murray said he knew the burglar. Alan reported the incident to the police, and whilst going through the investigation he admitted to a relationship with Murray. Both men were charged with "gross indecency" under Section 11 of the Criminal Law Amendment Act 1885. Alan accepted chemical castration as an alternative to imprisonment! Heart-breaking. This is a dark moment in UK history, because a man who had so much humanity within him couldn't be treated or seen as a human himself.

In retrospect, we can see the differences he made, and the achievements he made for later computer science. But his achievements were largely unknown in his own lifetime, his involvement was kept a secret under The Official Secrets Act.

Alan sadly died by cyanide poisoning. An apple was half eaten on his bedside table, this was suspected to be the means of his death. He died on the 8th of June 1954, in his house at 43 Adlington Road, Wilmslow. An inquest was held the following day which determined the cause of his death to be suicide.

I am a speculative person myself; I believe many factors play into the reason behind his death. I imagine the pressures of society, and the law having Alan be chemically castrated likely played a significant role. I won't say my speculation is truth, but it would be hard to deny the idea. At the end of the day, only Alan will know his own truth. I hope he knows he is not seen as the scum of society, as the law made him out to be, under the Criminal Law Amendment Act 1885. As mentioned earlier, the law was not changed until 1967 in the UK.

It is ideas and stories like these that show us why things needed to change. Alan Turing was a hero, and he still is! But everyone, regardless of "worth", are deserving of being treated like a human being. At the end of the day, Gay Liberation is a movement by humanity for humanity! This is but one reason why we needed the change. Thankfully we are more accepting today.

Musically, the 60s at face value would be rather void of Gay values!? But this is only at face value, dig a bit deeper and you'll find that this distinction becomes less distinct. Collectively, the ones who managed the music stars of the 60s era were, by an outsized margin, gay men and women. Such people like Vicki Wickham, who booked the acts on the seminal TV show 'Ready Steady Go' and who later managed Dusty Springfield and LaBelle. Then Brian Epstein (who brought to the world the Beatles), Kit Lambert (who co-managed The Who), Simon Napier-Bell (The Yardbirds, and a young Marc Bolan aka T-Rex), Robert Stigwood (Cream, The Bee Gees), Billy Gaff (Rod Stewart), Ken Pitt (David Bowie), Barry Krost (Cat Stevens), as well as Tony Stratton-Smith (who formed the visionary label "Charisma" for bands like Genesis). But these rich, powerful and influential men faced personal consequences. Being gay during the 60s was against the law for the most part, society itself was lagging far behind even when the law did change.

For America we have such people like Clive Davis at Columbia Records, Seymour Stein at Sire, David Geffen at Asylum and also Danny Fields.

A fantastic book if you find this side of the 60s valuable: "The Velvet Mafia: The Gay Men Who Ran the Swinging Sixties" By Darryl W. Bullock.

Some of the music associated with the Gay Liberation is not as vast as the later 80s era, but it can be found none the less during the 60s and 70s:

"You've Got to Hide Your Love Away" – The Beatles 1965
"Try For the Sun" – Donovan 1965
"You Don't Have to Say You Love Me" – Dusty Springfield 1966
"Emmie" – Laura Nyro 1968
"Walk On the Wild Side" – Lou Reed 1972
"Arnold Layne" – Pink Floyd 1967
"David Watts" – The Kinks 1967
"Lola" – The Kinks 1970
"(Sing if you're) Glad to Be Gay" – Tom Robinson Band 1976
(These songs are on that Spotify playlist again, check it out.)

Summary:

Gay Liberation was and still is a wonderful aspect of humanity. Whilst social change was being formed in support of society as a whole during the 60s, as we have seen, another concept was also being formed in support of society on a more individual sense. Rather than supporting everything all together as a whole, some people felt a new approach may be more fruitful.

Chapter 4

The Human Potential Movement

The Human Potential Movement or HPM was formed with a perspective to offer individuals the support and development that each person needed individually. The long term goal incentive was to help people access their own fullest potential in a deep and meaningful way. Through the development programmes that the HPM could provide, their idea was to enable someone to experience a life of joy, happiness, fulfilment, meaning and creativity. This belief that someone could experience such a life individually would assist a then positive change on society as a whole. 'A better individual, a better society' ethos. Through self actualisation an individual could then access their own fullest potential and become content with their lives.

This was also coinciding with a shift in favour of spirituality and meditation, which became very popular during the 60s era. The HPM wanted to support spirituality, spiritual enlightenment, psychological well-being and what it meant to be human. To ask such questions like 'who am I?', 'what is my purpose?' and 'what really is my fullest potential?' An almost philosophical question at this point.

So, how did the HPM begin?

One cannot talk about the HPM and not say it began without the Esalen institute in Big Sur, California.

The Esalen institute was set up in a unique way by Michael Murphy and Dick Price in 1962. The Esalen Institute building was owned by Murphy's family. Before the two set up the Esalen Institute, it was originally a hotel that went unused. Murphy's grandmother at the time still owned it but lived 60 miles away from the property. It had bath tubs that were being frequented by either homeless people, or by homosexual youths.

Murphy had approached his grandmother before on occasion to acquire the property, but she didn't want to give it to him as she was afraid, he, in her words: "Would give the Hotel to the Hindus."

(For context on what I will write next: Mr Thompson was a security man who patrolled the property with a firearm at the time.) Murphy at a later time commented: "Not long after, Thompson attempted to visit the baths with friends and got into a fistfight after antagonizing some of the gay men present. The men almost tossed him over the cliff."

Murphy's dad who was a persuasive lawyer managed to convince his mother to lease the property to his son, in hopes it would end the issues the property was posing at the time. Luckily, she agreed!

Dick Price and Michael Murphy themselves had developed an interest in human psychology and earned degrees in the subject in 1952. Their intention was to support alternative methods for exploring human consciousness, and what Aldous Huxley described as "human potentialities". They wanted a place to explore these alternative ways of learning, teaching and aspired to be free of the standard dogmas of typical educational programmes. After the lease was agreed, they incorporated their business as a non-profit named 'The Esalen Institute' in 1963. Price and Murphy weren't alone, they were given support by Frederic Spiegelberg, Alan Watts, Aldous Huxley and his wife Laura, as well as Gerald Heard and Gregory Bateson.

In 1962, Alan Watts presented the first lecture, I imagine this was whilst the property was still being refurbished.

Like Alan Watts himself in the 60s, many other people who came to present varying lectures or meditation practices were all influential figures within society. The institute went on to spark the foundation of the Human Potential Movement. By the middle of the 60s, George Leonard, an editor for 'Look' magazine ran an article on this newly emerging human potential movement. He carried out research across the United States on the subject of human potential. In his research, he interviewed 37 psychiatrists, neuroscientists and philosophers. He found and stated:

"Not one of them said we were using more than 10% of our capacity."

We aren't using more than 10% of our brain's capacity is a statement that has stuck with our society ever since, even if we don't link it to the 60s era.

Upon further research, Leonard came across this new Esalen Institute. George Leonard and Michael Murphy became close friends, and together "Put forth the idea that there should be a human potential movement."

By the early 1970s there were an estimated 150 to 200 growth centres modelled after the Esalen Institute throughout the United States. The Human Potential Movement was a success and seemed to be very popular.

The HPM outside of America

The HPM didn't really happen outside of America until the late 60s. There is very little information regarding the human potential movement in Europe. In the United Kingdom, the HPM began with such organisations as 'Quaestor'. It was a self development initiative loosely based on its American counter part, it was the first growth centre in the UK. Quaestor was part of the 'Encounter movement', which was a trend towards the formation of small groups in which various techniques, such as confrontation, games, and re-enactment were used to stimulate awareness, personality growth and productive interactions. These groups were held by individuals who had heard of, or at least learnt about the varying aspects associated with the HPM in America.

The 'professional scientific census' in the UK became more focused on Humanistic Psychology, this was an original growing branch from the HPM that was gaining considerable traction. There are several key theorists that have been considered to have prepared the grounds for humanistic psychology. These include Otto Rank, Abraham Maslow, Carl Rogers and Rollo May. It was referred to as the 'Third Force' because it represented an alternative to the two prevailing psychoanalytical and behaviourist methods of the time. The Encounter movement soon faded away though and evolved a path towards a variety of non-traditional therapies. These included Gestalt therapy, psychodrama, transactional analysis and primal scream therapy. The HPM also embraced a number of disciplines and practices (both Eastern and Western) involving; healing, self-improvement, self-awareness, and also included Zen Buddhism, astrology, art, dance and a variety of systems regarding body movement and manipulation. The more 'eccentric' aspects of the HPM have largely been compared to the short lived crazes of the 1960s and 1970s, such as primal scream therapy, but has still continued in varying forms to this day.

Elizabeth Puttick wrote in the 'Encyclopaedia of New Religions' stating:

"The human potential movement (HPM) originated in the 1960s as a counter-cultural rebellion against mainstream psychology and organised religion. It is not in itself a religion, new or otherwise, but a psychological philosophy and framework, including a set of values that have made it one of the most significant and influential forces in modern Western society."

One noticeable development here with the human potential movement, is that it shows a blend or flow of one social ideal into the next. I will try to explain this flowing development here:

The Beatniks were one of the first to advocate for social change, but stayed by and large a literary movement, so wasn't too political when it began. Then we have the Hippie movement, which evolved to suit many different types of social change, but developed into a largely political outfit, in a way branching out from the original Beat movement. Following on from these two, we then have the Human potential movement, which could see that society was changing legally for individuals as a whole, but it didn't change, help nor assist the Individual person. The Esalen Institute saw this as an issue, unsurprisingly.

Summary:
All of these social movements seemingly flow from one to the next, going from strength to strength. The HPM was encouraging the involvement of self help and guidance, so it's no surprise psychology was being introduced within the HPM as well. But again, a flowing narrative of change, revolution and evolution was less than immediately obvious at the time. No-one knew the future, we still don't today either.

Psychology remained as a progressive evolution outside of the HPM. It encased many triumphs and changes as well, the 60s so far seems to be full of change and development! The human potential movement is perhaps one of the remaining positive aspects of the 60s counter-culture movement.

Chapter 5

Ψ

Psychology and spirituality

Psychology:

The 60s saw a large shift around how we dealt with and viewed psychological wellbeing. What was occurring prior to the 60s needed to change, the framework that was being challenged by respected psychologists by the early to mid 60s was behaviourism.

Behaviourism

Prior to the 60s the most dominant form or framework towards psychology was called Behaviourism, it was championed by psychologists such as John B. Watson (1878–1958) and B. F. Skinner (1904–1990). Behaviourism was the scientific study of behaviour, it was hoped that laws of learning could be derived that would promote the prediction and control of behaviour. Russian American physiologist Ivan Pavlov (1849–1936) introduced and popularised early behaviourism in America, he provided support for the notion that learning and behaviour were controlled by events in the environment, thus it could be explained with no reference to mind or consciousness. Perhaps a very scientific approach if any?

Roll on into the 60s and psychologists began to recognise that behaviourism was unable to fully explain human behaviour, this is because it neglected mental processes. "Radical Behaviourism" was being used in the early to mid 20th century. This behavioural approach was introduced by B.F Skinner, Radical Behaviourism is rooted in a theory that behaviour can be understood by looking at one's past and present environment, looking at reinforcements that are within it, thereby influencing behaviour either positively or negatively.

The criticisms arise because people find issues with how a person themselves can cope with the events that are either good or bad, behaviourism can't explain this.

Cognitive Psychology

Bring in Cognitive Psychology, which was and still is known as "The Cognitive Revolution" during the 50s and 60s. It began in the late 50s and took hold during the 60s, when authors and psychologists started to implement this new framework into their practice.

During the 1960s, the Harvard Centre for 'Cognitive Studies', and the Centre for 'Human Information Processing' at the University of California, San Diego, were both influential in developing the academic study of cognitive sciences. It also helped to develop a new field of science known as "Computer science". Developments in computer science would lead to parallels being drawn between both human thought and computational functionality, similar ideas to that of Alan Turing and his 'Turing Test', or his 'Imitation Game'. This opened entirely new areas of psychological thought.

Prominent figures of this newly emerging field were Allen Newell and Herbert Simon, they spent years developing the concept of Artificial Intelligence (AI) and later worked with cognitive psychologists regarding the various implications of AI. This was prior to the internet or social media age we see today! In retrospect this was revolutionary.

Regarding Cognitive Studies, psychologist George Miller's 1956 article "The Magical Number Seven, Plus or Minus Two" is one of the most frequently cited papers in psychology.

This early development was largely based on the scientific method of mental processes, some observers have suggested that Cognitive Psychology became a movement during the 1970s.

Humanistic Psychology

The cognitive revolution wasn't the only psychological change to occur during the 60s, Humanistic Psychology was also taking shape around the same time.

Humanistic Psychology tried to rebel against the two main theories: Sigmund Freud's Psychoanalytic Theory, and B. F. Skinner›s Behaviourism, the two leading schools of thought. We now have a gentleman called Abraham Maslow who was a leader in a newly emerging movement known as the "Humanistic Movement". Maslow suggested and advocated for a 'Third force' in psychology, in addition to Behaviourism and Psychoanalytic theory.

It was made popular in the 1950s by the process of realising and expressing one's own capabilities and creativity. Because of this, it became popular with the Human Potential Movement, which was also roughly occurring at the same time. Abraham Maslow created and introduced his theory, "Hierarchy of needs". It is a theory of psychological health predicated on fulfilling innate human needs in an order of priority, culminating in self-actualization.

I cannot talk about Humanistic Psychology without mentioning Carl Rogers. Rogers is known especially for his person-centred psychotherapy; he wrote 16 books and many more journal articles about it. It is based directly on the "phenomenal field" personality theory of Combs and Snygg from 1949. Rogers is known for practicing "unconditional positive regard", which is defined to mean the accepting of a person "without negative judgment of .... [a person's] basic worth".

Fritz Perls is another gentleman, he coined the term "Gestalt therapy" to identify the form of psychotherapy that he developed with his wife, Laura Perls, during the 1940s and 1950s. He was also involved with the Esalen Institute because of his unique psychotherapy work. The central idea of the Gestalt therapy process is enhanced awareness of sensation, perception, bodily feelings, emotions, behaviour, freedom and self-direction all in the present moment. Because of this he was very popular and largely available at the Esalen institute, he was living at the property in the later half of his life until he died in 1970.

Perls has been widely cited outside the realm of psychotherapy for a quotation that is often described as the "Gestalt prayer":

"I do my thing and you do your thing.
I am not in this world to live up to your expectations,
and you are not in this world to live up to mine.
You are you, and I am I,
and if by chance we find each other, it's beautiful.
If not, it can't be helped".
—Fritz Perls, Gestalt Therapy Verbatim, 1969

1968 – Founding of the "Association of Black Psychologists"

This is a professional association of African American psychologists, founded in San Francisco in 1968, with regional chapters throughout the United States. It was formed not long after the assassination of Martin Luther King Jr. and the rise of Black Nationalism at the time. Ebony Magazine's publication of "Toward a Black Psychology" by Joseph White in 1970 was a landmark in setting the tone and direction of the emerging field of Black Psychology. (Ebony is a monthly magazine with Its target audience being the African American community.)

Due to the horrendous issues the Black community was facing during the 60s and elsewhere, many black psychologists united across the country. Their aim was to directly support those in need by people who knew first hand the issues their clients were facing. At African American Psychologists they wanted to create a positive impact upon the mental health of the national Black community by means of planning: programs, services, training and advocacy.

On their website: (https://abpsi.org/about-abpsi/) under their "Mission and Vision" section they write:

"The Association of Black Psychologists sees it's mission and destiny as the liberation of the African Mind, empowerment of the African Character, and enlivenment and illumination of the African Spirit."

It wasn't just educated 'white' people who made 60s Psychology worth talking about, visionaries such as the many who work for and set up this association are just as much the reason also!

Summary:
Many psychological benefits occurred during the 60s for many people regardless of heritage, many contributions I've mentioned so far in this chapter have made our understanding towards psychology vast and grand. Today, neuroscience is enjoying tremendous interest and growth, Psychology is ever expanding and growing. We face a need to de-stigmatise our public opinion towards mental health, a side to life we are all involved with.

Spiritually:

The 'New Age' Movement.

The new age movement, along with related terms like 'new era' and 'new world' have widely been used to assert that a better way of life for humanity is dawning. The expression "Age of Aquarius" within popular culture usually refers to the heyday of the hippie and New Age movements in the 1960s and 1970s. Traditionally, Aquarius is associated with electricity, computers, flight, democracy, freedom, humanitarianism, idealism, modernization, nervous disorders, rebellion, nonconformity, philanthropy, veracity, perseverance, humanity and irresolution. 'New

Age' is just a term to associate a range of spiritual or religious practices and beliefs, which rapidly grew in Western society during the early 1970s, unifying Mind, Body and Spirit.

The song "Aquarius/ Let the Sunshine In" by 5th Dimension – 1969 could be typically linked to this movement and the age of Aquarius.

New Age as a term. Alice Bailey born in 1880 was one of the first writers to use the term "New Age", she wrote over 25 books during her lifetime on theosophical subjects. The seven rays of energy, Esoteric healing, Esoteric astrology, The Constitution of Man, The Great Invocation, Discipleship and Service and Unity and Divinity of Nations and Groups; were all her top main theory's. Bailey was born in Manchester, England, living a life being educated in Christianity. She became involved in evangelical work with a connection to the YMCA and the British Army. Due to this she moved to India and met a man who would become her husband. They both moved to America, here Bailey became an Episcopalian priest. She had 3 children, but the marriage went sideways and didn't last. She left with her three children after their formal separation in 1915, followed by a difficult period in which she worked in a sardine factory to support herself and her children. Two years later she discovered the Theosophical Society and decided to join. She went on to form "Lucis Trust" in 1922 after falling out with the Theosophical Society. Her earlier work cemented her as a trusted member of this new religious movement. One of the many 'New Age' movements.

I might say this New Age all began in America, but to say this is being too specific, it arose from the 60s and it's influences such as the UFO religions of the 1950s, the counterculture of the 1960s and also the Human Potential Movement of the same era. Traditionally rooted in occultism of the eighteenth and nineteenth centuries, including the work of Emanuel Swedenborg and Franz Mesmer. Esoteric thinkers who influenced the New Age include Helena Blavatsky and Carl Jung.

Helena Blavatsky born in 1831 was a Russian American mystic and author who co-founded the Theosophical Society in 1875. Religious studies scholar Robert Ellwood explains here:

"Blavatsky is one of the most significant, controversial and prolific of modern esotericists. It is more than evident that, whatever one thinks of the more flamboyant aspects of this remarkable and many-sided woman, she possessed a keen intellect and a wide-ranging vision of what occultism could be in the modern world."

The Theosophical Society was and still remains an unusual 'cult'? or religious/ spiritual organisation. It was self-described as "An unsectarian body of seekers after truth, who endeavour to promote brotherhood and strive to serve humanity."

Blavatsky went on to inspire many people, her work helped to vitalise the 60s new age movement to no end.

Carl Jun, born in 1875 remains a hugely popular Swiss intellectual, author and psychologist who founded Analytical Psychology. My goodness, I find it difficult to really pin him down as a man, where do I start?!

A dream analyst, he put together a hugely popular collection of 'aspects' about and on the topic of our human psyche. I will list the names of these 'aspects'. Although I won't explain what they are or what they mean, I highly advise you look up and understand him for yourself because your interpretation will be different from mine. Hence not explaining what these aspects mean, because the meaning will be different from one to the next.

Anima and Animus — (archetype), Archetype, Archetypal Images, Collective Unconscious, Complex, Extraversion and Introversion, Persona, Psychological types, Shadow—(archetype), Self—(archetype) and Synchronicity.

All I can suggest is this, if you fancy losing yourself to a good weekend, look up his theory of "Collective unconscious", for me it is very similar to but not quite the same as the Buddhist theory of 'Ālaya-vijñāna', meaning 'storehouse consciousness'.

Onto the UK, many new smallish groups started to appear, branded as "The Light Movement", influenced strongly by the Theosophical ideas of Helena Blavatsky and Alice Bailey. Glastonbury is a village and civil parish in Somerset, England, which remains in our 21st century as a "Hippie" village. Another place in the UK is Stonehenge, this is a prehistoric megalithic structure on Salisbury Plain in Wiltshire, this is also attended by 21st century 'Hippies'. Both places are connected to the "New age" movement.

Now onto the very chilly North of the UK, we find Scotland. Home to the Findhorn Trust established in 1962. It formed into a trust as more people joined the original group consisting of; Eileen Caddy, Peter Caddy and Dorothy Maclean, who had arrived at the Caravan Park at Findhorn Bay. The trust boomed popularity during the ensuing 60s, with both the counterculture and the Hippies who were looking for new answers, they were inspired by the Findhorn Trust. Due to its popularity it became the 'Findhorn Foundation' in 1972, this was due to the community membership, which grew to roughly 120 members. The Findhorn Foundation is one of the many aspects of this spiritual movement, so is very much worth mentioning.

What can be said for both America and the United Kingdom is the New Age would vitalise many former members of the counterculture and Hippie subcultures, many of whom subsequently became early adherents to this 'New Age' movement.

So, over to America for the New Age. We have the Human Potential Movement, San Francisco Zen Centre, Transcendental Meditation, Soka Gakkai, Rastafari, The Inner Peace Movement and The Church of All Worlds. Regarding these differing avenues many of these new developments were variants of Hinduism, Buddhism and Sufism. They had been imported to the West from Asia following the U.S. government's decision to rescind the Asian Exclusion Act in 1965, which helped to boom these interests. Many famous people became wonders for explaining and exploring these Eastern philosophies, religions and ways of thinking/living.

Alan Wilson Watts (6 January 1915 – 16 November 1973) is perhaps the most celebrated and famous translator for these Eastern traditions. He is a gentleman who is celebrated for popularising Eastern thought for a Western audience, becoming a highly popular figure amongst the rising counterculture of the 60s. He was involved with the Esalen Institute in Big Sur, California, giving lectures on topics about Buddhist, Taoist, and Hindu philosophy. He was born in South East England, but became hugely popular in America, he wrote "The Way of Zen" published in 1957, which was one of the first best selling books on Buddhism at the time.

Alan Watts remains legendary today amongst those who liken to his messages of wisdom. Alan was very ahead of his time, he recorded many of his talks and lectures. Because of this, his popularity has grown on the internet, his son Mark Watts has worked incredibly hard to transfer these old recordings using old technology, but then onto new technology. This is great for podcasts and modern society. During the early 70s, it was suggested between Alan and his son Mark to create an "Electronic University" using his recordings. "Courses on Cassette" was the first offering of his recordings for the public in 1975. This wasn't long after Alan Watts passing in November of 1973.

Alan was increasingly concerned with the ethics we applied to our relationships between humanity and the natural environment, but also between the governments and its citizens. He coined a term "Organism-environment" where he saw neither the person nor environment are separate from one another. I have studied him for writing this book, my own opinion on Alan is he's the real life version of Zhuang Zhou or Zhuangzi, a Chinese Taoist writer/philosopher. But I mean that with the utmost respect to Alan, his family and his followers. Hopefully you'll understand where I am coming from when I say this, both of these figures are wonders for society.

Alan is criticised by many, which isn't shocking, he reaches so many people, not everyone likes the same thing. The criticisms I encounter reflect upon him that his work didn't go into depth about the varying Eastern philosophies or religions. He wanders off into a tangent at times and people feel as if he's leading you somewhere but isn't. His knowledge of Eastern thought is criticised also.

I can answer some of these issues, the typical recorded sessions on YouTube are usually a mixture of more than 1 lecture, it isn't surprising the majority of his work is seemingly therefore misleading. His knowledge isn't that wrong, because he states himself that he is a "Philosophical Entertainer" only wanting to share what he found interesting with others. My advice is to listen to the recordings created by the Alan Watts Organisation. His son Mark Watts has joined the "Be Here Now" network on Spotify. Through my research on this book, I used the Spotify recordings from the Be Here Now network. Here you will find Alan as he was without the annoying dubstep or chill step music over the top of his voice. So, whilst he has been criticised, his wisdom has changed an incredible amount of lives for the better, the messages of love, compassion and understanding on the varying social media platforms suggest that these criticisms aren't entirely correct.

Because his message at the time was captivating, he spoke to many noted intellectuals, artists and American teachers in the human potential movement. He was also welcomed by followers of Zen, such as Shunryu Suzuki, the founder of the San Francisco Zen Centre, who also welcomed him.

Alan wrote a substantial number of books, lived on a house boat called the 'Vallejo' situated in Sausalito, California, and also in a secluded cabin in Druid Heights, on the southwest bank of Mount Tamalpais situated north of San Francisco.

What can I say, he's someone who lived a fascinating life. His messages I hope will continue to change people's lives for the better. We all could do with connecting to nature in the now, caring more about the planet, ecology, the human spirit and the wider message of nature as a whole. Alan Watts, need I say more? I won't tell you to like him, make your own mind up. But start with his own work by his own family. The Alan Watts Organisation (AWO) it is the best place to start.

Bob Marley is perhaps an unlikely hero to place here under 'spirituality', but here we are, the 60s was an unusual decade, huh?

Bob Marley was a member for some years of the "Rastafari" movement. Because it is a new religion formed during the 1930s, it gained increased respectability within Jamaica, but found greater visibility outside of Jamaica, through the popularity of Rastafari-inspired reggae musicians, most notably, Bob Marley. So, Marley made Rastafari popular, Rastafari made Marley popular, win/win. What may also have helped make the religion popular during the 60s was the principal ritual of Rastafarians to smoke ganja, also known as marijuana or cannabis. Marley supported the legalisation of cannabis or "ganja", which Rastafarians believe is an aid towards meditation, a connection with a personal "higher consciousness" towards the divine and also a ritual for grounding.

Bob Marley lived a colourful life, but unlike a typical philosopher, he didn't attend lectures, seminars or talks, he wasn't Alan Watts with a guitar in other words, his message was his music, Reggae music! During 1963, Marley and his friends Peter Tosh and Bunny Wailer started a ska band called The Teenagers, before renaming themselves The Wailing Rudeboys, then The Wailing Wailers, and finally The Wailers. Bob went on to create fascinating music as a band, but also as a solo artist. I don't need to explain his legacy, he explains it himself in his music.

In the UK, Benjamin Zephaniah was a yet to be found dub poet (Dub poetry is a form of performance poetry of Jamaican origin) he wrote a letter to Marley along the lines of:

"I'm a poet from Birmingham. Nobody's really listening to me in England. What do you think of my poems?"

Unbelievably, Zephaniah received a hand-written reply from Bob Marley, all the way from Jamaica. The musician told him:

"Young man, Britain needs you. Keep doing what you do."

While Zephaniah revealed an 'English Heritage Blue plaque' at 42 Oakley Street, London, 2019, Zephaniah said that the letter was one of the main reasons he felt encouraged to pursue "dub poetry", the style for which he is now most famous for.

"It really inspired me to keep doing what I was doing, at the time there was no spoken-word poetry, there was no dub poetry, so to read those words…"

Bob Marley is surely credited with inspiring a generation of black British youths as well as many people world wide with his universal message 'One Love' and a unity for humanity. His album Exodus, released in 1977, had messages of peace and unity. Beauty was and still is his message, being the messenger, he has become and still remains the message himself. Exodus and One Love/People Get Ready was released in 1977.

Creating beauty in the world is what Bob Marley was all about, there is the iconic photograph of Bob Marley uniting the hands of Michael Manley and Edward Seaga at the 'One Love Peace Concert' in Kingston, Jamaica, 1978. A moment that was his attempt to rescue a socialist political movement in danger. During the mid to late 70s the democratic socialist People's National Party (PNP) and the conservative Jamaican Labour Party (JLP), were locked in an urban paramilitary conflict that killed, injured, and displaced thousands of people. Marley hoped through uniting the leaders' hands whilst creating music, he could show that the power of music and unity was more than just a gimmick. This event could have started a civil war in and of itself, but his perseverance managed to break through and show the power that people possess within themselves. That I believe is one hell of a message!

In essence, Marley introduced the world not only to Jamaican Reggae music, but also to Rastafarianism, it was rooted in ideas of personal and spiritual freedom, peace, love and cultural unity. A unifying concept of Rastafari was the saying "I and I" to mean whilst we say you, me, them, they and other, we create a gap between one another by doing so. "I and I" means we are in essence all one, without any division.

If "New Age" religion was to have achieved anything, I reckon it meant to have achieved just that!

The songs I feel I want to add here are:

"Within You Without You" – The Beatles 1967.

This Beatles song on their iconic album 'Sgt Peppers Lonely Heart Club Band' was written by George Harrison. The song musically evokes the Indian devotional tradition, but the blatant spiritual quality of the songs lyrics reflects Harrison's influences of Hindu philosophy, and the teachings of the Hindu Vedas.

"Exodus" – Bob Marley 1977.

"One Love/ People Get Ready" – Bob Marley 1977.

These two songs reflect the significant changes Bob Marley was making, both socially and musically. The album Exodus seems to revolve around themes of change, religious politics and sexuality.

Summary:
Psychology, spirituality, religion and everything else "new age" remain influential today. These changes truly kick started our modern era that we all identify with. Many psychological and spiritual developments have taken place since the 60s. Psychology is a strong component to our modern world, many people today are struggling to cope with mental anguish. Likewise, spirituality and religion are trying to fill a void within our society. Our secular age seems to neglect the strengths that come along with personal connection. Overall, the 60s was a vibrant time of change, positive change. I believe these positive changes could benefit us today, and they should remain within our social conscious awareness. We may just need these benefits to our society, now more than ever.

But, these changes during the 60s had an unusual trippy aspect…

Chapter 6

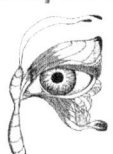

Psychedelics, LSD and conscious awareness

Notable figures here are Timothy Leary and Ram Dass (born Richard Alpert). Ram Dass and his book 'Be here now' helped popularise Eastern philosophy, spirituality and yoga. He remains a fascinating figure with many recorded lectures, ones that can be found via the 'Be Here Now' network. His work is accessible to many people, it requires little in the way of using mysticism, if that is an issue.

During 1960, Timothy Leary and Ram Dass were both Harvard professors who began to explore human consciousness with the aid of L.S.D (Lysergic Acid Diethylamide). But over a series of events, the two split up due to personal differences and opinions. Ram Dass was growing tired of being unable to sustain the awareness that LSD provided. He went on a search for alternative ways to achieve this state, without drugs. This issue of drugs being unable to sustain a prolonged awareness, it proved to be an issue amongst intellectuals and philosophers throughout the 60s.

Their work helped to popularise the use of drugs, allowing many individuals a potential way to enter so called 'spiritual awakening' or 'enlightenment'. This simple and easy idea went a long way in the 60s. It started to become noticeable within music and art that a shift towards spirituality and conscious awareness had taken place, but also in drug use. Popular bands such as The Beatles and their use of Eastern instruments in their songs, and the band members involvement with spiritual teachers, were clear indicators that a shift in focus was indeed taking place. The Grateful Dead was another band that was born out of this cultural shift in favour of drug use, spirituality, Psychedelics, or for the benefit of the counterculture itself specifically. It is difficult and perhaps controversial to pin down the Grateful Dead to any specific paradigm.

Psychedelic Art and Pop Art underwent a shift, fashion shifted and bands vinyl covers were used as an expression of self. This in and of itself was a reflection that changes in focus were actually happening.

These new and diverse drugs weren't just for the party goers though, or for the individual looking for enlightenment, it's uses were evaluated in favour of medicine and or psychological well-being. If they were used in a controlled environment, their effects on patients with P.T.S.D and other mental health concerns were certainly positive, and this was just the beginning. But not a great wealth of research was able to take place. The law changed banning many different types of drugs, potentially to deal with the party goers who were causing problems, or in worst case situations resulting in death. By the 1970s, the 'War on Drugs' was officially established. Many of these drugs benefits, especially to science, were lost to fear, law and public opinion.

The war on drugs

President Richard Nixon on October the 27th, 1970, signed into law the 'Comprehensive Drug Abuse Prevention and Control Act', 1970.

At a press conference on June the 17th, 1971, President Nixon, and his newly appointed Drug authority at his side, declared drug abuse "public enemy number one." "In order to fight and defeat this enemy," he continues "it is necessary to wage a new, all-out offensive." With that statement, the "war on drugs" officially began.

This had a significant cultural impact towards public views and opinions on drug use, but also towards those that use them and negatively stance addiction. Billions of dollars were given to support any anti-drug activity by police forces in Latin American countries, including Colombia, Peru and Bolivia. The drug war has been widely criticized by such organizations as the 'ACLU' for being "racially biased" against minorities and has been "disproportionately responsible for the exploding United States prison population". In turn, the war on drugs has also had a significant effect towards scientific studies, this is on drug use with patients who have mental or physical issues. The war on drugs has focused its efforts on forbidding the use of drugs and pushed a focus towards punishment, rather than complimenting regulations and treatments instead. These issues have coincidentally boomed the black market, and at times provided conflicting claims by a mixture of governments, its critics, academic studies, public opinion and news reports having a general mixture of statistics. These conflicting claims have proven to muddy our concept of addiction, well-being and other theories towards drug use. Un-regulated organised crime groups are in control of the black market, which leads to waste chemicals used in drug manufacture being illegally disposed of, often into waterways or on land in ecologically vulnerable environments. This is also a negative effect of the war on drugs and its wider reaching influence.

In the UK, the war on drugs founded The Misuse of Drugs Act in 1971. This surpassed the earlier Drugs (Prevention of Misuse) Act of 1964, which controlled amphetamines in the United Kingdom in advance of international agreements, it was later used to control LSD. Critics have cited that there was too much focus on arresting drug dealers, but not enough on treating the addiction that made drug dealing such a lucrative business to begin with, a similar story in America.

But the war on drugs hasn't always been here, early advocates such as Timothy Leary, Alan Watts, as well as a host of other individuals have all tried to advocate for both the positive and negative attributes of drug use. One such advocate was Ken Kesey who became a cultural icon during the 60s, all of which occurring prior to the war on drugs. Their ideas were in support of positive theories for individual people, but also to help them reach a better mental state, allowing people to reach new heights of inner potential.

This was in light of, but in favour towards raising an awareness that drugs must be respected.

Alan Watts quoted that "When you receive the message, hang up the phone. For psychedelic drugs are just instruments, like microscopes, telescopes and telephones. The biologist does not sit with his eye glued to the microscope, he goes away and works on what he has learnt." Quote from Alans lecture: "Drugs: Turning the head or turning on."

I must say the lecture is an incredible insight into the 60s era, and the views towards drugs of that time by people of society.

With our modern hindsight, the war on drugs has somewhat proven that our current political approach has been a failure. Perhaps the idea to spread awareness of drugs in both a positive and negative light, socially and scientifically, would have been a more fruitful endeavour? In some way the counterculture may have actually been right in the first place, their views on drug use and ideas to raise an awareness about them, both positively and negatively, may have saved the government trillions? Controversial to suggest this perhaps, but it is also controversial what the government's reaction to drugs has been.

Unfortunately, the media at the time painted the Hippies as dark figures, and the ensuing 70s war on drugs victimised those using drugs, especially minority groups. Today we cannot see the Hippies or other such groups during the 60s without having a negative or put down mind-set towards them. This seems to only further distance and negatively stance our perception towards what the Hippie stood for, forcing us to only see them as dirty, druggy, delusional, naive and spiritually or scientifically misguided with aspects like "Woo-Woo". But it has also darkened our view towards our social attitudes on drugs today. The government and their war on drugs has done many things, but in the wrong way.

Today we are professionally, scientifically and socially heading in a direction to undo what the government's have done previously. Boldly going to places that we were already heading towards prior to the war on drugs. As an example, cannabis has become legal in many states throughout America, so far it seems to be showing positive results, drugs can be used in a positive way, only if they are used consciously and respectfully. The idea was first suggested during the 60s era that things such as set and setting, who you are with and under what circumstances the drugs are being used or taken, this will alter their effects and the users experience. As they were saying in the 60s, drugs can be both good and bad, so respect must be given.

Medical cannabis, as well as other psychedelic drugs (some of which are also known as "Plant Medicine"), are being researched by scientists following on from the original work that began in the 1960s. The results so far have shown that many individuals can gain considerable benefits in various aspects in their physical and mental health. The research is ongoing, so what I may write as new today, will be old news tomorrow. For modern reference, I can point you in the direction of David Nutt. He is a fellow at the Royal College of Physicians, Royal College of Psychiatrists and the Academy of Medical Sciences. Being a Neuropsychoparmacologist he specialises in the research of drugs. He is an interesting man, so I suggest you look into him for further information and knowledge.

Psychedelic, psychoactive or plant medicine has given rise to many alternative life styles or ways of thought and practice. One such man who took it upon himself to live in an unusual way found drugs by accident. This man is Ken Kesey, a novel man shall we say, in more ways than one. Yes, my jokes are terrible... I'm here all weekend.

Ken Kesey and his famous "Acid-Tests":

Ken Kesey was a famous author during the 60s but during 1964 and onwards he became a cultural icon with his 'band of merry pranksters', who were a collection of close friends. They went on a grand trip, journey, exploration or whatever you feel fits, spreading the idea of love joy and of course LSD. (LSD wasn't made illegal until the 30th May 1966.)

To understand why Kesey became this cultural icon, we need to understand the events that lead up to 1964. What was happening during the time prior to Kesey becoming a famous author was of course the Vietnam War. The war was occurring afterwards as well but has a crucial element prior to 1964. America had concerns regarding the Soviet Union at this point prior to 64, an awareness to many potential issues regarding chemical, biological and radiological interrogation of their US troops. To better understand these methods of interrogation, America's CIA formed 'Project MKUltra'. The purpose Of MKUltra was to develop procedures and thus identify drugs that could be used during interrogations to mentally weaken people resulting in confessions through brainwashing and psychological torture. The CIA performed essentially illegal human experiments under the name MKUltra to better educate themselves about these potential risks.

So, with this mysterious and dark background, we can return to the jolly Ken Kesey. Roughly during 1958-59, Kesey elected to enrol in the non-degree program at Stanford University's Creative Writing Centre. Kesey was living next to a guy called Perry Lane who was noted to be a 'bohemian' living in an enclave next to the university golf course. Kesey frequently clashed with Centre Director Wallace Stegner, who regarded Kesey as "a sort of highly talented illiterate". During Kesey's 5 years as a student, Kesey was invited by this unusual Perry Lane figure, and a Stanford psychology graduate student Vic Lovell, to become a volunteer with an unusual psychological programme. Why Kesey agreed to attend the programme is speculative, I would say it may have given him a reason to write something, an unusual inspiration of some kind perhaps? But, unknown at the time, Kesey had volunteered to take part in what turned out to be the MKUltra programme. Kesey's role as a medical test subject, as well as his short lived job working at the Veterans' Administration hospital, both inspired his novel 'One Flew Over the Cuckoo's Nest'. Kesey released the novel in 1962, which was set in an Oregon psychiatric hospital, the narrative of the book was as a study of institutional processes and the human mind, including a critique of psychiatry, portraying also the boundaries between sanity and madness. The book is cited as his most famous novel, later being turned into a film based on the book itself. It goes without saying the novel was an immediate commercial and critical success when it was published. The film is the second to win all five major Academy Awards at the time during the 60s (Best Picture, Best Actor, Best Actress, Director, and Screenplay). Kesey was initially unhappy about the film, but later reflecting upon it in life, he said he was supportive about the project, he was just happy the novel was made into a film at least.

With the money he made through the novel, he moved to nearby La Honda, California, and began hosting "Happenings" with his former colleagues from Stanford. These happenings later evolved into the name "Acid-Tests", centred on the use and advocacy for the psychedelic drug LSD, commonly known as "acid", hence the name Acid-Test.

Now we know his involvement with this MKUltra programme, it likely inspired his interests in LSD and mind manipulation, possibly serving the basic concept behind these happenings or Acid-Tests. During this time period he wrote his second novel "Sometimes A Great Notion", published in 1964. This is where he becomes a cultural icon.

Kesey, a cultural icon.

Whilst writing his 2nd novel, and hosting these Acid-Tests, Kesey was building a customised large out of service 1939 International Harvester school bus, as you do. He built and designed it to be semi lived in, thus, to enable him to tour America. After the 1964 publication of his second novel, "Sometimes a Great Notion", New York required his presence, so he decided to use his new custom bus to take the long trip from La Honda to New York, a journey just shy of 3,000 miles (4828km).

As these Acid-Tests had proven to be successful so far at his home in La Honda, Kesey decided this trip should be an event in and of itself! Kesey and close friends Ken Babbs, Carolyn "Mountain Girl" Garcia,

Lee Quarnstrom, Neal Cassady and Tom Wolfe, collectively took up the name "Merry Band of Pranksters." Collectively they had the idea of turning their adventure into a road movie, taking inspiration from Jack Kerouac's 1957 novel "On the Road."

The bus was painted by artist Roy Sebern in Psychedelic colours, patterns and scenes, naming it "Furthur". Tom Wolfe chronicled their early adventures in his 1968 book "The Electric Kool-Aid Acid Test." Some of these antics and adventures can be seen and found on YouTube, if you wanted to see what happened. What becomes apparent is that the Merry Band of Pranksters were using LSD, including the driver Neil Cassady, but they didn't die, which I find to be a miracle really! Throughout their journey they met with many icons of the counter-culture movement, they did try to meet with Timothy Leary, but weren't able to do so. Ken Kesey stated that he wanted to be seen a link between the Beatniks of the 50s and the Hippies of the 60s. The Merry Band of Pranksters hosted many Acid-Tests using the Grateful Dead for their music at these events. The band itself 'The Grateful Dead' were known originally as 'The Warlocks' in their early days. As the news spread about this epic trip, many found inspiration in what Kesey was doing and what he was advocating for, thus he became a 60s cultural icon.

One song that comes to mind about this trip written by The Grateful Dead is "Truckin" from their album American Beauty, released in 1970. Although Truckin wasn't actually inspired by these events, the song that was apparently inspired by these 1964 events with Ken Kesey is "The Other One". According to Bob Weir, he wrote the lyrics to The Other One apparently out of pure inspiration given by the Furthur bus, which the lyrics refer to. The lyrics are here as follows, see if you can make any links after reading this short summary of Ken Kesey's cross country adventure:

"Escaping through the lily fields, I came across an empty space.

It trembled and exploded, left a bus stop in its place.

The bus came by and I got on, that's when it all began.

There was Cowboy Neal at the wheel of the bus to never ever land."

Ken Kesey without a doubt managed to popularise the use of Psychedelic drug use but did it in such a unique way that the youth of the time became fascinated with the idea. Word of mouth likely mystified what happened, how it happened and what these drugs actually do, or did. Suddenly, people became interested!

Kesey remained a cultural icon until he died on the 11th of November 2001.

Psychedelic Music

These events of 1964 with Ken Kesey's cross country adventure likely sparked a new movement of Psychedelic music, or at least an interest in experimental bands. The leading band of this type of music was indeed The Grateful Dead but isn't exclusive to just them. In the UK we have Pink Floyd, they were and still are a unique band.

The music centred on mind perception-altering hallucinogenic drugs. The music was used as an alternative way to allow the listener to experience altered states of consciousness, depersonalisation, de-chronicization, and dynamization, all of which detach the user from their everyday reality. Why people wanted to escape reality is up for debate. Either personal issues or social issues at large, either one could be correct during the 60s. But, considering the cultural issues of the time, this form of new escapism became hugely popular. An escape from reality wasn't the only benefit these hallucinogenic drugs seemed to provide, many used the drugs as a form of musical experimentation, mysticism, ego death, or for pure recreational use.

The music was embraced by the Hippie movement of course, as were the drugs that came along with them. So, people who weren't Hippies during the 60s and also people today connect the idea of a Hippie simultaneously with drug use. But ironically, the Hippie subculture was vast and grand, those who simply existed to use drugs were in and of themselves a minority group within the subculture itself, which was a minority group. What seemed to help infuse this connection between drug use and Hippies was the media.

A social conscious awareness towards the use of drugs was wide spread, not just exclusive to the stereotypical counter-culture movement. It encapsulated many academic studies, peaked scientific interests and helped towards a better psychological understanding. So, drugs at the time sat outside of the Hippies and their "noisy weird music".

The peak years of psychedelic rock during the 60s were between 1967 and 1969, with milestone events including the 1967 Summer of Love and the 1969 Woodstock Festival. Both of these cultural events became infused with the 60s counterculture, because they were the counterculture. But those musical icons associated with our widespread counterculture began to decline along with our changing attitudes. The loss of some key individuals, and a back-to-basics movement led surviving performers to move into new musical movements. Society was also growing up, so musical tastes started to change, Crosby, Stills, Nash and Young are a band that had a more 'mature sound' to their music as an example of this change.

Some of the songs that go hand in hand with this Psychedelic counter-culture movement are listed below:

"Truckin" – The Grateful Dead
"The Other One" – The Grateful Dead
"Can't Come Down" – The Warlocks
"Incense And Peppermints" – Strawberry Alarm Clock
"Time Of The Season" – Zombies
"I Had Too Much To Dream (Last Night) – The Electric Prunes
"Cream Puff War" – The Grateful Dead
"Lucy In The Sky With Diamonds" – The Beatles
"Killing Floor" – Jimi Hendrix
"A Whiter Shade Of Pale" – Procol Harum
"Purple Haze" – Jimi Hendrix
"Wooden Ships" – Crosby, Stills and Nash
"Magic Carpet Ride" – Steppenwolf

"Suite: Judy Blue Eyes" – Crosby, Stills, Nash and Young
(These songs are also on that Spotify playlist)

Summary:
The psychedelic era of the 60s has changed the face of society, both positively and negatively. The positives have certainly been felt within the music scene, spirituality scene, philosophy, and sciences. But the negatives have mainly been within politics, or political attitudes towards drug use. This unique aspect of the 60s has certainly been trippy.

But for the counterculture itself by 1967 a big "Happening" was going on. An event called "The Summer of Love" was forming, where roughly 100,000 people in support of these newly emerging movements headed to places where it was indeed "Happening".

Places such as Haight-Ashbury in San-Francisco, where the biggest number of people gathered together was the epitome of such change. It was a cultural utopia, all forms of music, hallucinogenic drugs, civil rights, free love and anti war were all evident. Other areas such as NYC and Denver had a summer of love going on too, just not in as many significant numbers like San-Francisco. All together it was considered a large cultural event, by even today's standards. These milestones in cultural history of course included these psychedelic drugs and the music that was inspired by them. But I would need to do an entire chapter on just the 1967 Summer of Love, so much happened in such a short amount of time.

Going forward by two years,1969, we land at the Woodstock Music and Arts Fair 15-18th of August. A music festival with as many as 400,000 people, one of the largest festivals held in history. Almost similar in design to that of Glastonbury, which is held in England today.

32 acts played here despite adverse rain, but no violence whatsoever occurred, suggesting that a real life event that should have gone wrong, if these people were actually 'bad folk', but it didn't. Many regard the event as the height of the counter-culture movement. The site remains in tact still today being kept as a museum as 'Bethel Woods Centre for the Arts'.

Chapter 7

The 'Happening', society and the Summer Of Love, 1967

For many people by 1967, the importance of personal wellbeing, spirituality and new ways of life and living saw an ever increasing number of people actively searching for new answers, meaning, purpose and fulfilment.

Because of this cultural search, what happened in the summer of 1967 is like nothing we have ever experienced since. America subsequently saw an influx of counter-cultural people from all avenues of life. They mainly gathered at Haight-Ashbury, San Francisco and other places such as New York City and Denver.

Meanwhile in the UK, the "Love-In Festival" at London's Alexandra Palace (Ally Pally) drew massive crowds to watch bands like Pink Floyd, The Nervous System, The Apostolic Intervention and many more. The UK by contrast to America wasn't quite so rich in a wash of Hippies, love, peace and music. These times in the UK are largely over shadowed by the American version where "The times they are a-changin" was evident. Regardless, the UK was certainly going along in the same flowing narrative or ethos that the Summer of Love encapsulated.

Some critiques say the Summer of Love was sensationalised, without cultural benefit, or it wasn't as much of a big deal as people say it was. But regardless, it still managed to bring together over 100,000 people to Haight-Ashbury, it changed music and really gave people hope at a time when life really lacked that aspect. The music was incredibly expressive, new, unusual, psychedelic and groundbreaking. The Beatles Sgt Peppers Lonely Harts Club Band album had an immediate cross-generational impact. The album was associated with numerous touchstones of the era's counterculture, such as fashion, drugs, mysticism, a sense of optimism and also empowerment. It was one of the first successful "Concept albums", or what we now call them today, all because of the Beatles and their innovative ideas.

In the UK during 67, nothing could have captured this Hippie ethos or the embodiment of the Summer of Love like the UFO club did in London. The club was established by Joe Boyd and John "Hoppy" Hopkins. It featured light shows, poetry readings, well-known rock acts such as Jimi Hendrix, avant-garde art by Yoko Ono, as well as local house bands, such as Pink Floyd and Soft Machine. Pink Floyd had arranged the first events, which combined live music with light shows, avant-garde films and slide shows. But, due to Pink Floyds growing popularity, they didn't stay for long. Hopkins and Boyd settled on Soft Machine as a replacement, but also started booking other acts who were attracted by the club's reputation at this point.

1967 Social Media? Magazines were the original social media of the era. Published in London from 1967, "Oz" was a popular alternative/underground magazine associated with the international counterculture of the 1960s. Originally it was an Australian magazine, but in early 67, Richard Neville and Martin Sharp (editors for the magazine in both the UK and Australia) came to visit the UK. With fellow Australian Jim Anderson, they founded the London Oz. The magazine, proving to be very popular, regularly upset the British establishment with a range of left-wing stories that cited heavily critical coverage on the Vietnam War, the anti-war movement, discussions of drugs, sex and alternative lifestyles.

Some noted that Oz was rather "intellectual", so the 'International Times' (IT) was a decent alternative. Editors of IT included John "Hoppy" Hopkins, David Mairowitz, Roger Hutchinson, Peter Stansill, Barry Miles, Jim Haynes and playwright Tom McGrath. Paul McCartney donated to the paper as did Allen Ginsberg with his 'Committee on Poetry' foundation, both real icons of the era, so this made IT a must have.

A song called "The Letter" by the Box Tops, was a number 1 top hit in the USA and number 5 in the UK charts. Wayne Carson wrote "The Letter", he built on an opening line suggested by his father: "Give me a ticket for an aeroplane". It was a unique song, with no defining riff, it couldn't be classed with any specific genre like blues, jazz or rock. This song is one of those indicators that life was indeed changing, but it couldn't clearly be defined. It also reflects upon the era also, no one really knew where things were going or heading.

During the 1960s, the Beatnik writers engaged in a symbiotic evolution with freethinking academics including the experimental psychologist Timothy Leary, which brings us to the beginning of 1967.

Now, the Summer of Love begins most certainly in the Haight-Ashbury district of San-Francisco in January of 1967. Hunter S. Thompson termed the district "Hashbury" in The New York Times Magazine. Newsweek printed a four-page four-color "Dropouts on a Mission" and Time magazine printed an article "Love on Haight". But it wasn't the mainstream articles that drew original attention to the San-Francisco district. Allen Cohen, the papers editor and Michael Bowen the art director were among the founders of "The Oracle of the City of San Francisco", also known as the San Francisco Oracle. They both published an advert stating:

"A new concept of celebration beneath the human underground must emerge, become conscious, and be shared, so a revolution can be formed with a renaissance of compassion, awareness, and love, and the revelation of unity for all mankind."

It was an advert for "The Human Be-In", which was an event held in San Francisco's Golden Gate Park, Polo Fields, January 14, 1967. This event held quite the message for the counterculture which was one of; Personal empowerment, cultural and political decentralization, communal living, ecological awareness, higher consciousness (with the aid of psychedelic drugs), acceptance of illicit psychedelics use and a radical New Left political consciousness. Quite the counterculture really.

It was at this event that Timothy Leary set the tone and voiced his now famous phrase: "Turn on, tune in, drop out". Leary explains the term in his 1983 autobiography in 'Flashbacks: A Personal and Cultural History of an Era':

"Turn on" meant go within to activate your neural and genetic equipment. Become sensitive to the many and various levels of consciousness and the specific triggers engaging them. Drugs were one way to accomplish this end. "Tune in" meant interact harmoniously with the world around you—externalize, materialize, express your new internal perspectives. "Drop out" suggested an active, selective, graceful process of detachment from involuntary or unconscious commitments. "Drop Out" meant self-reliance, a discovery of one's singularity, a commitment to mobility, choice, and change. Unhappily, my explanations of this sequence of personal development are often misinterpreted to mean "Get stoned and abandon all constructive activity".

The Human Be-In was announced on the cover of the fifth issue of the San Francisco Oracle as "A Gathering of the Tribes for a Human Be-In". Timothy Leary was joined by Richard Alpert (soon to be known as "Ram Dass"), with poets like Allen Ginsberg, who chanted mantras with others such as Gary Snyder and Michael McClure. Other counter-culture icons included comedian Dick Gregory, Lenore Kandel, Lawrence Ferlinghetti, Jerry Rubin and the philosopher Alan Watts.

I mentioned earlier about the song "The Letter" by the Box Tops, but the song was one song amongst many! Local rock bands were amongst these icons including Jefferson Airplane, The Grateful Dead, Big Brother and the Holding Company, Quicksilver Messenger Service and Blue Cheer, most of whom had been staples of the Fillmore and the Avalon Ballroom. The Fillmore was an incredibly vibrant, well known and stable of the Haight-Ashbury music scene. The Avalon Ballroom was a smaller venue, but still incredibly popular. A song by Big Brother and the Holding Company referenced the Avalon Ballroom in their song "Combination of the two", introducing the female vocalist Janis Joplin, many people had never heard of her before 1967.

The Monterey Pop Festival was the moment that made Janis Joplin famous, as it did for other artists like Jimi Hendrix, Otis Redding and more. "San Francisco (Be Sure to Wear Flowers in Your Hair)" was a song expressing the life and times of what was going on in Haight-Ashbury, it was written by John Phillips of the Mamas & the Papas and sung by his friend Scott McKenzie. It was produced and released in May 1967 by Phillips and Lou Adler, who used it to promote their 'Monterey International Pop Music Festival' held later in June. The Monterey Pop Festival was planned in seven weeks by John Phillips and others. It was a three-day music festival held on June 16th – 18th, 1967. Their ambition was to create an event that was multi-cultural, multi-national and multi-genre. The festival attracted 200,000 people, being it was the first true "Rock Festival" of America, it was quite an achievement. Please watch any videos of this festival on YouTube or whatever you can, truly it was an iconic event, second only to Woodstock during the 60s. Jimi Hendrix received national attention, as did Janis Joplin, The Who and others. All artists who were relatively unknown prior to the festival in America. Otis Redding wasn't that well known among white audiences prior to the event, so this changed things for him also. Others who played at Monterey included Jefferson Airplane, Simon & Garfunkel, Canned Heat, Al Kooper, The Paul Butterfield Blues Band, Quicksilver Messenger Service, Hugh Masekela, The Byrds, Booker T & the MGs, The Blues Project, Grateful Dead, Buffalo Springfield, The Electric Flag, and The Association. What make up, outfit or style would you go for if you were going to such an event? I'm a guy and even I'd wear make up, I don't care!

For the Human Be-In event, my goodness, the national media was stunned! The publicity about this event led to the mass movement of young people from all over America to descend upon the Haight-Ashbury district, just to see if any of it was actually true. They wanted to see if it was "Happening".

The Summer of Love 67

The Summer of Love is optimised as an eclectic mix of varying social movements varying from the anti-war, anti-Vietnam, civil rights, spirituality movements and more. All of these aspects collectively descended upon the Haight-Ashbury district of San-Francisco. This allowed many things to occur that wouldn't have done otherwise for many individuals. It did show our society that things can work between one another, love was all you needed, but it gave a real sense of power to the people. People felt that they themselves really could make the change, which was a powerful motivator for many of these movements. This mind-set reflecting against the Vietnam War was a real chalk and cheese scenario. Hope seemed to be on the horizon.

The Vietnam War is perhaps one of the main driving forces of this counter-culture movement. It was yet another war that the world didn't need, but it was still enduring, it seemed like a pointless war for many people by the late 1960s. Those who were drafted to the war and coming home were ridiculed for having been involved by many young kids, this negativity badly effected the mental well-being of those who had fought in war. So, there was a fear developing that was felt by the many young collage student's who didn't want to become involved. Many Veterans returned with PTSD, so, who wants PTSD for no good reason? By 1967, the war had reached a point where Americas involvement was at it's peak with Vietnam and it was showing. The war was a political action against the Soviet Union, where the North and south of Vietnam was occupied by different political powers. The South was aided by America and other anti communist allies, the north was driven by the Soviet Union, China, and other communist states. In January of 1967, 32% of Americans thought the U.S. had made a mistake in sending troops to Vietnam. This growing opposition to the Vietnam War was partly attributed by the greater access to uncensored information, mostly through extensive television coverage on the grounds in Vietnam. This exposure through television was something previously non-existent, so, during the 60s it was an entirely new concept. This new exposure gave the general public direct access to what war really looked like, what ugliness it had to show us, and how seemingly unnecessary it all was; all whilst people were having dinner at home with their kids.

This might be where it ends right, people dislike the war, people oppose the war and job done, but no. This open exposure to the war unsurprisingly caused people to become distrustful towards the 'Establishment' itself, forming an Us against Them mind-set, an almost good vs evil attitude. This is quite understandable though, many who opposed the war and made their action against it were relatively young people. This mind-set has stayed with our society since the original 60s era. It has become almost second nature to many people that feel a dualism with themselves and any form of Establishment, there is an Us as a society, but then the 'Establishment' as completely 'other' or opposite aspect. This dualistic nature I personally find is a downside to the 60s counterculture, where for many, but not all, they were becoming increasingly involved with Eastern philosophies, spirituality practices and religions, which actually promote a non dualistic approach to life, it is ironic. I find this personally troubling regarding the counterculture movement, so is a negative aspect of the 60s counterculture.

But on the other hand, I am also sympathetic, because I can see how well loved and respected the establishment was for many people up to this point. How dare they be involved in such a situation, one that 'the people' themselves disliked. But also, how much money it was all costing.

The idea that such a trusted establishment would do such a disservice to the nation and its people was troubling for many, so why would you see them as a fellowship any longer? This is perhaps a question I cannot answer here, it sits with those who are psychologists or philosophers. Perhaps even if you did see the Establishment as on your side at the time, maybe you were outnumbered by those who didn't? Thus, the bias lies prominently towards a dualistic mind-set of us vs them.

Considering all of these points, the Vietnam war was a hot topic as were the many social justice campaigns. The effects of what was occurring at the time had a profound effect on music, art, cultural perspectives and fashion.

The Hippie movement itself was in full swing by 1967, some say it began in 1964, so it was still relatively new by 67. Reflecting upon the counterculture movement in its entirety, you could see the Hippie subculture accounting for either 100% of the movement, or only accounting for possibly 25% of the overall movement. The reason between the two percentages comes down to our personal perspectives.

What may help us here is to ask what the Hippie values were and what they consisted of? But their values weren't only restricted to protecting and uplifting other humans, and protecting mother nature in any way hippies could. They also had a back to the land narrative, protect other animals by eating a vegetarian lifestyle, stop wars as this damages other people and the planet. They also encapsulated freedom, humanitarianism, idealism, modernization, rebellion, nonconformity, philanthropy, veracity, perseverance, humanity and irresolution.

These values would account for 100% of the 60s counterculture movement, because the Civil Rights Movements, Women's Liberation Movement, Gay Liberation Movement, anti-war protests, a back to the land ethos, environmental concerns and animal welfare concerns all fit into this 'Hippie' narrative. So, it comes down to opinion for how much of the counterculture we assign to the 'Hippies'. So, with this insight, we may agree that the hippie subculture is 100%. But would those people within the Civil Rights Movements call themselves Hippies, as an example? This is when we realise the issue in naming and using sweeping generalisations to cover the entire movement as a 'Hippie' movement. Yes, Hippies existed as people who advocate for these changes, but the movement's themselves wouldn't identify as being the 'Hippies'. Perhaps the 'true' Hippie is actually the original Beatnik, because of the similar values and philosophies held between them, but then again, a difference can be drawn between the Beatnik and the Hippie. Perhaps the Hippie is a social concept, idea or ethos? One that did indeed exist during the 60s, but it would only account for a maximum of 25% of the overall counterculture movement. Again, it comes down to our personal perspectives on what we call a Hippie? Who were the Hippies? Perhaps this is a difficult or tricky question to answer upon reflection.

I'm writing a book here on the 60s counterculture, and even I would struggle to give a true definition of what the 60s Hippie even was, where do they fit into society and how much of society accounts for the Hippie? It isn't so easy when we are seriously asking how Hippies fit into it all. I felt it necessary to add this in here, as many people may not even ask this question.

Let me try and flesh this out here, the 'Hippie' might actually just be a name for a state of being, or for a particular set of values. Each individual held differing values depending on many, many variables. So, the question "What is a Hippie?" is actually difficult to answer without using sweeping generalisations. All too often today, the Hippie of the 60s is seen as being naive or hopelessly optimistic, which again is a sweeping generalisation, it does little to serve as any truth. Some people were naive, absolutely, young people surely can be. What this sweeping generalisation seems to have done though is it has soured the taste of what the Hippie was, is and will ever be. Today it is better to be "woke" than "Hippie", which ironically is and was what the Hippie embodied, to a certain extent. If we changed the name from '60s Hippie' into '60s Woke', what happened during the 60s makes just as much sense either way. But what changed over time was our cultural perspective towards what actually happened, and who by.

The Hippies regarded modern life during the 60s as a soul-less, runaway machine. They viewed society through the philosophy of the Beatniks and other varying aspects of Eastern spirituality and meditation. They held an open oneness with nature and with other people. Vegetarian diets became very popular because of this awareness to nature needing to be "saved" or "protected". All too similar to our views today, but we don't identify with a social construct called 'Hippie' any longer.

During the 70s, less than 10 years later, 'Sentientism' was formed. It is an ethical philosophy that grants moral consideration to all sentient beings, not just humans. 'Sentience' is the capacity to experience suffering and or flourishing. Perhaps this has something to do with the Hippie narrative, or their ethos in some way towards protecting and considering all life on Earth. But today, being a Hippie is seen as being naive, perhaps this generalisation has done more damage than originally intended?

Hippies might have said at the time something like: "We would do well to put Mother Earth ahead of shopping/consumerism! And we need to drive for peace, love and unity in all aspects of life. Our care, love and drive to improve the world for humanity and animals would essentially attain peace." Again, this is ironically seen today as a naive outlook in some way. This view we hold today against the Hippie subculture of the 60s almost suggests that we hold the same views as the mass media of the time. Many people in today's society hold a negative connotation against the Hippie movement, such negatives as "drop out", "druggies", "dirty" and "social outsiders", reflecting the same narratives and opinions that the mass media had during the 60s. Perhaps it is true in many ways, but let us say that no culture is perfect, it just depends on how you look at it, but also from what vantage point. Are we actually holding different values today than the Hippies did of the 60s?

What I find occurring during 1967 is helpful for us today. Avoid using mass media without consideration towards what is useful, true and or challenging to our belief systems. Perhaps make our own media that does reflect the true situation, one that covers aspects we can all benefit from, much like they did with Oz and IT.

Perhaps 'Love is all you need'? A popular slogan made by the mega band The Beatles during 1967. Well, I'm not keen on this slogan, as it is far too open to interpretation. I would say a non-dualistic view of seeing both love and hate in the world, seeing how we reflect upon these two aspects of love and hate as one whole mutual thing. One cannot exist without the other. Love isn't all we need; we also need an element of the opposite also. This is a controversial idea, but when we reflect upon the values we hold today, is it really all that controversial?

Yes, the 60s counterculture movement might have been naive in many aspects for some people, but it is too easy to say this with hindsight/ retrospect, it is also too easy to cast sweeping generalisations as I hope to have pointed out. We would have done the same as they did during the 60s if we could swap places with them, especially without any hindsight to guide us.

Some of the music I feel is significant of 1967, which reflects this significant change in society I will list below. I could list many more here, but I've only chosen a select few:

"San-Francisco (Be Sure To Wear Flowers In Your Hair)"
– Scott McKenzie – 1967
"The Letter" – The Box Tops
"Combination of The Two" – Big Brother and the Holding Company
"White Rabbit" – Jefferson Airplane
"Get Together" – The Youngblood's
"A Day In The Life" – The Beatles
"Light My Fire" – The Doors
"Fire" – The Jimi Hendrix Experience
"Let's Live For Today" – The Grass Roots
(These songs have been added onto the Spotify playlist.)

Summary:
1967 was a huge driving force for many people to change the world, themselves and society. It was a social positive change that made many things happen in a good, significant and measurable way for those people alive at the time. In retrospect, such things like the contraceptive pill may have done more damage than we think. I feel the issues of the contraceptive pill needs to be spoken about more in our society today. Was it as positive as it seemed to be during the 60s?

1967 wouldn't have been much without the involvement of the peace sign though, which isn't what most people think it means.

Chapter 8

A symbol of peace, the Hippie peace sign

The peace sign, it is perhaps seen by many as the embodiment of a representation and motivation towards, well, peace. Some people have the symbol made into a tattoo, others feel it represents the Hippie motto or ethos, some people may not even care. But the symbol is actually connected to a much darker aspect of our society, a much more destructive origin than driving towards peace, an origin that is linked to World War 2.

During World War 2, humanity had formulated and created the atomic bomb, many tests were performed in aid of research, and to search for the effects of such a weapon and what it could achieve. At this point, if you haven't watched it already, I would suggest watching a film called 'Oppenheimer', or perhaps read the book, this may give you a more insightful view into what occurred during the 1940s era.

During WW2, 1945, Germany surrendered on the 8th of May, this led to the allies turning their full attention towards the Pacific War. This war involved some of the largest naval battles in history, including huge allied air raids over Japan. Tensions were certainly high, but when the consent by the United Kingdom was obtained for atomic bombs to be used by America, as was required by the 'Quebec Agreement', the orders were issued on 25th July by General Thomas Handy, the acting chief of staff of the United States Army. This was an all new style of offensive against Hiroshima, Kokura,

Niigata, and Nagasaki. So, on the 6th and 9th August 1945, the United States sent and detonated two atomic bombs over two Japanese cities, Hiroshima and Nagasaki respectively. Only these two cities were ever bombed though, this was because, for the first time, atomic weapons were used against fellow human beings, instead of buildings and dessert landscapes. The devastation that the two bombs caused was like nothing anyone had ever seen before, marking a new era of warfare. The two bombs killed between 129,000 and 226,000 people, most of whom were civilians. This ultimately led to Japan's surrender, but it has had people divided on ethical and or philosophical foundations. Some on the one had agree the bombs may have saved many lives by stopping the war itself, others on the other hand say that nuclear weapons are unethical, regardless of the situation. Unsurprisingly, many people tend to lean towards atomic weapons as being unethical. For me, atomic weapons are unethical as it effects more than just human life. Nuclear war would end more lives than just human lives.

What atomic weapons represented, quite clearly, was for the first time in human history, a message needed to be acknowledged: on the one hand, they are a huge achievement of humanity, science and ingenuity. But on the other hand, atomic weapons also represent the horrific reality that humanity could bring about its own end, a message for humanity by humanity.

For many people, this awareness to a potential deadly reality, it naturally caused panic and deep fear. Now, many of those who could in the UK, formed the Campaign For Nuclear Disarmament (CND). This fear and sensational reaction turned the minds of many towards pessimism.

Following WW2, it is fair to say that the whole of Europe was gripped by the very real fear of nuclear conflict, asking questions such as: who possesses these bombs? Who could, who would, and finally should we own these bombs ourselves?

Tensions ran high, a huge meeting formed by the CND was held in London in February 1958, to discuss these issues. Following on from this meeting, many marches were held to showcase the new CND symbol for the first time. The symbol was designed by Gerald Holtom during the 50s, it used a superposition of the semaphore signals and letters "N" and "D", taken to stand for "Nuclear Disarmament." The CND symbol, aka Peace sign was formed.

Because nuclear weapons pose a threat to everyone, regardless of their varying walks of life, the CND received sympathy from many, many people. Scientists above all were the most aware of these threats that lay ahead with nuclear weapons. Even influential people of faith became vocal about their support towards the CND movement, Canon John Collins of St Paul's Cathedral was one of these many influential people. Even a highly educated philosopher became involved in the campaign, Bertrand Russell.

Now going into the 60s, the 'Committee of 100', led by the celebrated and admired philosopher Bertrand Russell, was set up to organise mass civil disobedience. This platform of peaceful protests to raise an awareness towards a particular issue, well, it went a long way during the 60s era, that's for sure. The Civil Rights Movements adopted this idea of civil disobedience, for the most part, it proved to be a great success.

The concept of civil disobedience caused a problem for some, many felt the line between legal and illegal was a vague line. But for those in defence of such a strategy, they argue that it may be necessary to commit a lesser crime in order to prevent a greater one from occurring, such like nuclear war. So, in short, morality is a sticky issue and divides many on what to do.

This civil disobedience, regarding nuclear war, and feelings of nuclear anxiety weren't in vain though. The true threat of nuclear war was brought much closer to reality in 1962. The Cuban Missile Crisis rocked the lives of many, it wasn't a fanciful campaign any more, it was actually a true horror and true reality. This managed to exacerbate fear that nuclear war may indeed happen if we aren't careful. This real fear, caused by the Cuban Missile Crisis likely reminded many that life is not certain, it likely caused many people to re evaluate their lives.

Because these weapons posed a very real scenario that death is likely to come at any moment, especially if a maniac is in charge of a nation, or accidents were to occur, pessimism and anxiety grew stronger. This caused a considerable shift in favour towards living in the present moment for many people, but not to confuse this shift with spirituality, no, this formed an understandable mind-set where things in life need to happen now! Especially if anything in life is to happen at all. This is an unfortunate mind-set to hold, because it has likely brought about a rising popularity in consumerism, fast food chains and brash decision making, all without any long term initiative being considered. Perhaps a new social value formed here, we perhaps have now forgotten why it formed? Everything needs to be instant; food, travel, relationships, love and material things. How many things do we 'want' in modern society, which aren't connected to it being instantaneous in some way? Perhaps this want for instant things is linked to nuclear fear in an odd way?

I am sympathetic to why this mind-set was formed, because anyone today in a situation like that would live the same way also, yet in retrospect, it formed naive outlooks, and produced costly effects towards our future generations.

This 'living in the now' is ironic though, what people dealt with at work was the complete opposite of living in the present. This was due to a booming economy. This caused a forming mind-set or outlook that pushed job ethics and work models towards saying: "We have more in life yet to achieve, either a job promotion, better pay, a pension and or retirement. You see, happiness comes from achieving work, money, material goods and more". These things can only be achieved by working even harder, so we work hard and aim for these things in life that can only be attained in our future. As I say, it is rather ironic, it is because this pushes people away from the here and now, we forget the present moment in favour of the future. It is ironic as nuclear war pushed people to be aware of achieving things in the now, and only in the now. Confusing huh?

So, whilst the fear of nuclear weapons caused many to live for the now, this 'now' moment could only be achieved later. It would be similar to me saying that time runs faster than you can, the more you run after the future, the further away it gets from you. This is also similar to the law of reversed effort (backwards law), meaning the more we try to succeed at something, the less likely we shall be successful. They were running after the future in reality, but they only saw and wanted to achieve a 'now' outlook. This is a great example of this backwards law theory. Unfortunately, many people at the time didn't realise this issue. What this did was help cement the idea that productivity is the only goal in life. Money is more important than wealth, productivity always comes before you, always. This ideology is still within our society today. Are you running after time, after the future? Time runs much faster than you can, productivity will lead you down a road that has no end.

Time itself has played a key role in representing the many issues of mankind, nuclear weapons posed perhaps the greatest threat to humanity during the 40s, 50s and 60s. In 1947, founded by Albert Einstein and former Manhattan Project scientists (those involved in creating atomic weapons) 'The Bulletin of the Atomic Scientists' was formed. It was a non-profit organization, concerning both science and global security issues.

The intention of the Bulletin was to educate fellow scientists about the relationship between their world of science, but also the world of national and international politics. In essence, the Bulletin was formed to showcase these socio-political issues. In 1947 a clock named "The Doomsday Clock" was created, it represents the likelihood of a man-made global catastrophe, it was formed by the wisdom and knowledge of the Bulletin of the Atomic Scientists.

The Doomsday Clock was set at 2 minutes to Doomsday (midnight) during the 50s, and then 7 minutes to Doomsday during the 60s. The clock can fluctuate as it is based upon politics, weapons, diplomacy, climate science and many other factors, some of which may be new threats that may occur in our future. Many of these issues get added onto the list as time goes by, thus it affects where the clock is set.

The symbol of the CND movement has, much like the Doomsday Clock, persisted through time. The symbol was adopted by the counterculture movements in the 60s, mainly because of the many Anti-war protests and campaigns that were being formed at the time. The CND symbol was against the Nuclear Atom Bomb, so it fits nicely within the framework of war in general, or that's how people saw it at the time. It has become mixed with ideals towards peace, harmony, love and as a symbol in opposition to war. This of course makes sense upon reflection, fortunately it has proven to enrich what the original symbol means.

War certainly seems to drag on through time, from roughly the mid-1960s, nuclear issues became replaced with the subject of mass popular protest for many over the United States' war on Vietnam. This stayed the same case until the Vietnam War ended in 1975, but, during 1979 though, there were nuclear issues again as America had deployed and stored nuclear weapons within British and European soil. Civilians felt they would become new targets in an issue they didn't want to be a part of. So, talk about the CND and their efforts were back once more. This flows the rivers of time now into the 1980s. On 26 September 1983, during the Cold War, the Soviet nuclear early warning system 'Oko' reported the launch of one intercontinental ballistic missile with four more missiles behind it, from the United States. These missile attack warnings were suspected to be false alarms by Stanislav Petrov, he was an engineer of the Soviet Air Defence Forces who was on duty at the command centre of the early-warning system. He hesitated to retaliate, waiting on corroborated evidence, rather than relying on the warning by the chain of command. This hesitation actually stopped the real situation of nuclear war, a rather significant moment in history. Perhaps another notable event during the 80s was the 'Greenham Common Women's Peace Camp'. Not surprisingly, it quickly became the focus and symbol of women's resistance to what many saw as the "male-dominated" world of nuclear weapons.

Going through time we are met with Margaret Thatcher, the first female UK prime Minister, she seemed to have embarked on an anti-Soviet, anti-communist crusade. The mind-set of this 'Us Vs Them' was back yet again, much like the 60s 'Us vs the Establishment'. A true good vs evil, God vs the Devil, an almost similar framework to Star Wars. I find sadly this mind-set is perhaps a downside to the 20th century overall. I will return to this damaging 'Us Vs Them' ideology within the remainder of this book, as we will see it has caused great damage. This leads us into the 21st century now.

For those interested in what might happen to us in the 21st century regarding nuclear war, I have a fascinating book to suggest: 'Nuclear War, a Scenario' by Author Annie Jacobsen published in 2024. It takes non-fiction data and information from many respectable perspectives but narrates the book as a fictional scenario should a nuclear war occur. It is a grim and horrific account of what would likely happen should the unthinkable ever become a reality. Brilliant book.

Time never stops flowing, even when we aren't watching. The CND still continues today, mainly because these threats remain present and remain a potential reality. But nuclear weapons are always evolving and developing, luckily the majority of British people remain against nuclear weapons, as does the rest of the world in general. Our concerns towards such an outcome are no less relevant today than they were during the 20th century. So, in short, the fears of those of the past are just as prevalent and real for us today, some things remain present even though the rivers of time have flown through many people's hands. It seems the power of the sun is in the hands of those who could end the world. I can understand why this image may induce a nihilistic mind-set and may have led many people to garner a skewed vision of reality, as I have outlined in this chapter. Do we live for the 'now', do we live for the future, or do we retreat in nihilistic apathy? This is a difficult question; we aren't the first to deal with such a situation. We are similar to those of the 20th century more than we think.

A mid 60s band called; The West Coast Pop Art Experimental Band released a song in 1968 called: "A Child Of A Few Hours Is Burning To Death". This song I believe is a bluntly political song but highlights a sinister outlook on war and social responses toward it. The lyrics "We should have called Suzy and Bobby, they like to watch fires," really adds a haunting layer of commentary on our society. It suggests we hold a disturbing, yet macabre fascination and or detachment from violence, with individuals preferring to witness the destruction from a distance rather than take action to prevent it. The song serves as a poignant reminder that urges individuals to confront uncomfortable realities of war, but to engage with empathy and action, rather than remain a passive observer. For me, this song overall is rather fitting upon reflection towards the CND movement and their message to take action, instead of remaining a passive observer.

"A Child Of A Few Hours Is Burning To Death" – The West Coast Pop Art Experimental Band.

Summary:
The CND symbol is far more than just a Hippie sign. The rich tapestry of nuclear war has woven many unhealthy mind-sets, leading them into the 21st century. Nuclear war isn't going away any time soon, it seems to be persistently gaining traction. As Jimi Hendrix said: "When The power of love overcomes the love of power, the world will know peace." Strikingly relevant for our modern world, as it was during the 60s era.

So, as time is now drifting away from the 60s here, how did the counterculture of the 60s come to an end?

Chapter 9

A coming end to the 60s counterculture

A quick Summary:

    The 60s counterculture was partly formed by the Boomer Generation, but was also a mixture of the previous generation, the Silent Generation. Collectively, they gave rise to the civil rights movements, the Anti-War movement, the Women's Liberation Movement, the Human Potential Movement and many other movements. All of which I have covered so far in this book. This was to give these movements some context and explanation, I hope. Many issues were raised and supported with people becoming both self aware and also socially aware of our many issues. The 20th century truly was the beginning half of our modern era of our so called 'social justice era'. The mid 20th century saw many social changes making it the peak of social change. Today, we are still a major part of that same process, even though we may think we aren't.

    Today, because of these varying changes, things like music, fashion, art and the way we now live have evolved beyond recognition, these changes have a lot to do with what happened during the 50s, 60s and 70s.

So, we could ask: were the Beatniks and Hippies successful?

Absolutely yes! They introduced new ways of thinking and managed to alter the way the world works, with their effects still evident today. People are still advocating for freedom of choice for who they want to be, but to be simultaneously free from prejudice. Although many things have indeed changed, I would say not all ideals were met.

So, the next question is: what brought the end to this change, revolution and social justice 'counterculture' of the 60s?

The peak of our social justice movement, or where the Hippies began to dissipate: First and foremost, the media coverage was a major contributing factor to the decline of the 60s counterculture. The easy target for the media itself was certainly these Hippie sub-cultures, in short, these sub-cultures were mocked and given a bad light. Anything that could hush away the Hippies was good press, anything that made out these kids to be ironically dangerous (when peace and love was their motto), dirty, smelly and so on was a good thing. Basically, anything that socially put's the counterculture down, seemed to be good media or press. This social change is now considered to be a much needed and shining light of human achievement, at least in retrospect. So, again, why was it put down if it was actually a good thing?

I will try to provide some context as to why this was the case; the 60s was the beginning of our modern social justice and self exploration movements. So, many aspects of our previous, or our pre-war social identity was being challenged and changed. This upset and directly challenged many people keen on holding onto our pre-war identity. Controversy makes good press, and with anything that is new and or different for our society, on the whole, these social changes are typically feared or challenged.

This fear becomes translated into mocking, sometimes violence, put-downs and also ridicule. The social counter response to (ironically) the counterculture, well, these many such changes can be tracked to what the media covered or portrayed. This reflects what our collective view towards such changes was like. What we can now learn today is that it offers an insight towards societies responses to such events, at least should something similar to the 60s happen again.

The eventual end of the Vietnam War helped to slow down the American counterculture, and it's further reaching influence. Because a large portion of the counterculture was opposed to the Vietnam War when the war itself ended, so did the need to fight and rebel against it.

In an odd way, what also aided the end of the counterculture was actually the counterculture itself. This was because many of the outlooks and mind-sets that went against mainstream culture, (hence counterculture) became more and more part of our mainstream culture and society. I went into how and why this was in the 1967 chapter, making us as a collective society the ideal hippie. So, it became less of a counterculture movement, but more of our culture itself. So, in short, it was no longer 'counter' any more, but just our 'normal' culture instead. So, the need for such a culture was less desirable, or even needed. There always remains a counterculture of sorts within society, but the specific 60s counterculture certainly dissipated. It has never truly disappeared entirely though, but this flame has been kept alight by the culture we live in today.

What was seen in the 60s was a shift in political outlooks, or social ideological groupings, such as left wing and right wing ideologies, the 60s Hippies were considered "New Left". Generally, the left wing is characterised by an emphasis on ideals such as freedom, equality, fraternity, rights, progress, reform and internationalism. The right wing is characterized by an emphasis on ideals such as authority, hierarchy, order, duty, tradition, reaction and nationalism.

Because of the influences created by the 60s counterculture, we now sit with a society that largely (but not entirely) sits in, and is built upon, many left wing ideals. This may strike people as shocking, but these "new left" ideals mainly control, or are a large influence upon the media we see today. This flipped around media response to these such cultural changes may be the definition of ironic itself. 60s media disliked the Hippies, but today's media generally supports the hippie idea, or left wing ideal. The 60s counterculture can be idolised and supported today by some TV media companies who hold left wing ideals, which really wasn't the case during the 60s. Often the 60s are seen today with rose tinted glasses by left wing idealists.

But whilst the 60s went through enormous social change, it wasn't without hardship, failure, misery and conflict, this must be remembered. Rose tinted glasses makes people lose sight of this aspect. Conflict and triumph go hand in hand when large social change is occurring, but because our left today is built upon the original left wing ideologies of the 60s, the view towards the 60s is seen and viewed as only a good thing. This just makes those in the left feel more special and justified. It is all social games, but it isn't entirely unjustified, we really did need these changes in the 60s. I don't want people to lose sight of how things actually were, reality is more interesting than fiction. War exists because of peace and visa versa. The 60s wasn't all happiness, sunshine and rainbows. The fiction misses out the fact that for many young people (but not all), it wasn't always a pleasant time. People died, family's fell apart and trauma occurred. These two factors of the bad and good need to be combined, appreciated and remembered, otherwise we will only see the good, thus have only good as a reference. But, aiming for mutuality between both will put society in a much better place, one compliments the other.

Another aspect of the coming end to the counterculture was yet again the counterculture itself. These people who made up the counterculture were growing up, they had to have jobs and they needed to earn money. But none of these kids were rich, they didn't have dad's money to help them in other words, many had to make and find their own way in life. This was the same for all the other aspects of the counterculture, not just exclusive to the Hippie sub-cultures, so, the Civil Rights Movements, the Women's Liberation Movements, Gay Liberation Movements and so on, they all had life which happened to them. This involved kids growing up, jobs to develop and attain and futures to attain. Just like us today, we deal with the same life challenges. This likely played a role in the decline of a teenage dream of social justice. During the 80s, a term arose to define this cultural change called "Yuppies" meaning "young urban professionals".

Now we can ask from the perspective of the modern 21st century, have these social changes gone away entirely? The answer here is absolutely no, but what has changed is that the counterculture is no longer seen as something new. The counterculture soon became old news, or perhaps better put, normal everyday news. So, we can perhaps ask something else; does the media cover the many Hippie communes, aspects and all the rest of it in the way they did during the 60s? The simple answer here is again no (I'm not including social media here, only TV media). This is because at the time during the 60s, these things that were occurring socially were relatively new for people. These social changes are now no longer new, so are boring, but these changes continue to evolve, yet they all stem out of these various 60s movements. They can be found on social media, if you look, but they won't be found on public service media any more (Aka; the TV).

This is a good place I would like to bring to light something, everyone today takes for granted the TV. This was fairly new technology for the 60s, so the type of coverage showcased on these new TV's was about the many different aspects of society, this is the same as we do with social media today, as social media is a new technology. What was shown on TV became popular coverage, it became an important medium to express what was going on in our society. Today, social media is just an extension of TV, it has only become a different platform to showcase our social changes. As society itself changes, so does our expression and depiction of it, thus what we see regarding our society changes, which is my point, it just becomes normalised.

So, we can also ask today; are the Civil Rights campaigns being covered in the same way as they were, are the gay liberation movements being focused on in the same way, the Women's Liberation or feminism, so on and so forth? For all of these cultural aspects, the answer still remains no. This is for the same reasons I have put forward so far, and that is because our society has evolved and changed. What was 'new' then, it isn't 'new' now, so these aspects get pushed aside in favour of something that is actually new today. What is being covered now has mainly been taken into the hands of our society itself. Such coverage is being done through social media, podcasts, YouTube videos and a whole host of other ways that are all different from the 1960s version (TV) but remains an evolution of the 60s era. No longer are these big TV companies in charge, we the people are the ones taking charge today. We evaluate, focus on and investigate our society, like we did during the 60s, our society evolves, and because of this, simultaneously, so does our way of expressing it and viewing it.

My own personal view today is that our overall cultural mind-set has been shifted in such a way that nobody pauses to question what life might look like had the 60s counterculture never happened? Some people may not even link connections between the 60s and our life today. But the short answer to this question "What would life be like if the 60s counterculture had never happened?" is; life today would be unrecognisable, simple really. Short and sweet, but what I hope to have pointed out are these many links and changes between us and, well, us. All we did was socially evolve, we didn't begin, end and start again, evolution doesn't work in that way.

The way we now dress, listen to and also play music, the way we feel about cultural differences and how we talk about sex at home is far more open, these are only some of the many aspects that have indeed changed, most of these changes are positive, but the mutuality remains in all things, others have also been negative. I would say that it is far better to be alive today though because of this, compared to what it was like to be alive during the 60s and 70s. Of course this is a debatable outlook to hold, and largely depends on where you live globally. China for example, is going through very, very difficult cultural issues that are mainly linked to its economy. So, of course what I say doesn't apply here in this case, it is a generalisation again. But in America and the UK, generally it is better to be alive today than it was during the 60s and 70s.

So, whilst things aren't being covered by the media in the same way as they were during the 60s, what made the counterculture in the 60s counter-cultural has now become part of mainstream culture today. This has un-doubtfully had an affect on the way we now view society. This is perhaps one of the biggest impacts that ended the 60s counterculture, the fact that what was counter-cultural is no longer counterculture, it just is our culture now.

So, something that happened during the late 60s, which contributed to the end of the 60s counterculture was a far darker side to humanity. It is more dangerous than just fearful media coverage, or the counter-culture ideals becoming part of our modern society. One of the least Hippie like people to walk the earth, a person who can certainly fit the definition of a "wolf in sheep's clothing", brought huge concern and fear towards the Hippie movement. This fear which caused oppression towards the Hippie sub-cultures, ideas that have stuck with our society ever since. The wolf in sheep's clothing was none other than Charles Milles Manson, (born November 12, 1934, Cincinnati, Ohio, U.S. — died November 19, 2017, Kern County, California). I won't go into the details of what he did here, as coverage on and about him is vast and grand. In short, he was an American criminal and cult leader whose followers carried out several notorious murders in the late 1960s. Their crimes inspired a best-selling book called Helter Skelter (1974). The effects of these notorious murders negatively effected societal views towards the counterculture itself. This also helped support the medias case against the counterculture, which had a knock on effect on how society (who weren't the counterculture) viewed counter-cultural people (mainly hippies). This was certainly another contributing factor towards the decline of the 60s counterculture. The counterculture could no longer be trusted with peace, love and freedom, all because "what if one of them is the next Charles Manson?" Fear is a dangerous thing; the media knew very well how to use it.

This leads me onto a profound and reality checking point to make: an Us vs The Establishment ideology.

To bring to light something different here, what society has perhaps not put together between the 60s counterculture, their US Vs the Establishment ideology and Charles Milles Manson, is that it actually played against the counterculture itself.

Let me explain:

The counterculture ideology of their US Vs Them was brought about via a distrust in the Establishment for various reasons, mainly because the Vietnam War was heavily criticised. This therefore pushed some people and their opinions about the Establishment in the wrong way. It became a political pursuit by people who weren't in political power to go against the Establishment. But this Us Vs Them mind-set actually backfired against the hippie counterculture. It is perhaps the most naive, dangerous and radical ideology to ever hold.

What brought about this reality that possibly any given hippie could be rather disingenuous, the same basic idea that was held against the Establishment via the hippie, was Charles Milles Manson. This gave a strange situation where this US Vs Them mind-set was held in both directions. Some of the hippie sub-cultures were against the Establishment, but likewise the Establishment itself was against the hippie movement, and because of this, the many that were in support of the Establishment also followed suit. This strange situation snowballed into the eventual demise of hippie sub-cultures. The hippie counterculture was outnumbered by those who weren't hippies. Sadly, this has led many to remain distrustful and dislike hippie folk today, even if those that hold a distrust against the hippie don't know the reasons why any longer. It has become normalised, forgotten, but still apparent.

This is perhaps where the biggest unseen irony here comes up. As I have mentioned before, a large portion of modern society is held together by a growing support of new left ideologies. Mainly because there remains a lot of clout that the left ideology holds. But what the irony is with this is, the left ideologies or 'new left' today is built upon the hippie sub-cultures of the 1960s 'new left'. So, although people may dislike the idea of the 'Hippie' itself, many people are hugely in support of their ideologies and worldviews, which creates a rather ironic situation.

Many hippies of the 60s would hugely support solar power, electric cars, wind farms or renewable energies, they would have supported recycling waste products, gender identity changes and more. Now, for me, these ideologies are rather obvious when we consider the ideologies that were held by some of the hippie counter-culture people of the 60s and 70s. But because these ideologies now come without the direct involvement of needing to identify as a 'hippie', these things have now become acceptable. Again, even though the hippie advocated for the world we live in today, they are seen as the 'bad naive people'. Therefore, those who drive a support in these ideals today could be considered 'left wing'. Again, our social spectrum has shifted to sit more in the left today than it has ever done before in history. Of course, many in the right wing are in support of such environmental changes and concerns, but I feel the guiding support is from those who sit within our left wing spectrum, or those who consider themselves centre point. But again, centre point would have been the original left during the 60s, unlike today. So, is the centre actually centre, or is it just seen as being right wing?

What isn't great about this spectrum today is that we tend to get many 'extremists'. Hopefully by expressing how the social spectrum has evolved, it may be easier to see how close the far left is, that is if we already sit closer to the left as a starting point. For some people, to appear as being 'left' today is to actually become 'extreme' left. This is because 'left' has lost it's meaning or has become skewed. This is to say, we all live naturally in a dominantly left ideology today, so to be left today, compared to the 60s left, is just to be a person who ventures into far left ideologies. Politics makes all the difference, either socially or within law.

Politics are where things see the most change, and this Us Vs the Establishment ideology, which I feel has stuck around, is getting in the way of things today. If we fight against those who can make the change by law, and make them the enemy, then this will cause a civil war, make younger people feel like the country isn't worth supporting, make young people feel like it is against them and more. This makes sense because why support a country that doesn't support you? Where do the incentives lay if we feel like the people running the show are the issue? This Us Vs Them will drive our society insane, nihilistic, isolated, indifferent and might even cause a civil war.

So, these are a few reasons as to why the 60s counterculture came to a close. What does this mean for us today then, really?

Chapter 10

What about today though?

Are we any different from the 60s counterculture, even with all these changes they made, and also with the changes that we've made?

Your first thought might be yes! (If we exclude the last chapter). Yes, we are very different from the 60s, we have mobile phones, no more hippies, (or at least a select few compared to then), we have better cars, even electric ones, we have better human rights for many people, even such things like gender equality and more. So, cultural things have changed and evolved.

But when we really think about the counterculture of the 60s, as explained so far, you realise that what the counterculture advocated for, it really isn't that far different from what we still advocate for in today's world. I admit that yes, while things like civil rights aren't as bad as they were during the 50s, they aren't where they could be today, but we have come a long way since the mid 20th century. So, some things have actually changed, we aren't an exact copy.

In a more poetic way to frame our modern society, in contrast to the society that has gone before us: 'An individual creates a society, a society creates an individual'.

These two are joined inseparably, one cannot exist without the other. But, if we only know of one half of this mutuality, more so 'An individual creates a society', then we will only understand the 'What' questions. Such questions like 'what' am I searching for, 'what' is it that has led us to our situation today, and 'what' on earth is going wrong with our society today? This will put people in the dark upon many aspects of their own lives, their place within it, and what this means to and for them.

But, if we know the mutuality and see that 'a society creates an individual', then we will understand the 'Why' aspects, in addition to the 'What' aspects. This will allow us to see more clearly the position we find ourselves in today, providing clarity instead of disparity. So, this is to say; our past is when many things began to change and influence further changes, thus it has created the foundation of our modern day society, and where we are culturally.

So, when we ask the 'what' questions of today, like what is meaning, value and fulfilment to mean in my own life? The other half is 'a society creates a person', which is the 'why' aspect. People will wonder 'why' they feel, lost, unsure, isolated and insecure, but the 'why' answers escape them, the why itself has no answer. If we can see a link between ourselves and 'a society creates a person', we can better understand these 'why' reasons. Thus, these feelings of being unsure, or even these feelings of anxiety will make more sense. We will have both the 'what' and the 'why' simultaneously in our modern era today.

So, what many people did during the 60s created our society, social foundation, and a reality that we are all a part of today. This same society that we are a part of today also creates the person who lives within it, how they can navigate around it and how they feel inside, thus creating a person and their values. These values then get reflected back out into society and the process begins all over again. "A person creates a society; a society creates a person" has never been so true.

The 60s was when many of these social changes began to take shape, but it didn't begin in the 50s and then end in the 70s, as we may often think, it actually began and has never ended. These issues are still relevant for us today, even though the 1960s began over 60 years ago.

War, civil rights, the environment, gender identity and many other aspects are still relevant today. I would go as far as to say that even more aspects have been added onto this original list. But these are considered by many to be good changes that our society needed.

But how long will a good thing last though, I don't know? I will expand upon these cultural issues later, these positive changes come with negatives. Essentially, one cannot exist without the other, positives exist because of the negatives.

So, when considering these cultural changes, the counterculture of the 60s becomes a lot more relatable and far less different or distant. So, in many, many ways what the 60s counterculture ideology was, has become what we now call normal, as explained in the previous chapter.

This isn't to suggest that everyone needs to wear bell bottom jeans, put flowers in their hair, or to become as stoned as possible, just like the stereotypical hippie seemed to be, or is now portrayed. But you can if you want, who cares?

Younger generation Vs older generation:

Seeing today's world in the way I have explained and expressed, this negative, naive portrayal of the hippie is almost ironic, especially when we today share their values. Yet this negativity is still present towards those of the past. So, how come? Do the younger generations tarnish the older generations with the same brush of negativity, not individually, but collectively?

Today, by some people, but not all, the Boomer Generation (born between 1946 – 1964) isn't seen in a very good light. One of the biggest traits associated with the Boomer is that of ignorant bliss, mainly towards global warming issues, peak oil, mental health and more.

Some people see the Boomer Generation as being typically in resistance towards technological advances and changes.

This is a quote I have created that would reflect a similar opinion held by some of our younger generation:

"For over a decade they've had to tug on the sleeves of someone younger, often a stranger, on an extremely regular basis asking for help with technological advances. They don't seem to want to even learn. Yet they brag about being the "toughest" and "greatest generation". They see us as the "snowflakes", how ironic"

This kind of view is held towards those of the older generations by people from mine (Millennial) and younger (Generation Z).

This negative view might be short sighted though. Many changes have occurred in a stupidly short amount of time, more and more technology gets changed and developed by default. As we know, old technology gets thrown away, or stuff comes and go's as 'fads' or 'trends'. This might be a difficult evolution to follow, deal with and cope with. Especially when older generations no longer value being 'in' with the 'in crowd', or latest 'fad' or social craze held by young people. Why be trendy with a generation you are no longer a part of? These older people have seen more fads come and go than any younger generation could sensibly deal with. For reference, read the entire first half of this book and choose anything from music, Mods and Rockers, Teddy Boys, spirituality trends and more, these things have all come and gone in various ways. The fact older generations seem disinterested, no longer value or cannot deal with 'our' fads and technological advances is almost obvious. They delegate these issues onto someone who actually cares or is trendy, the older generations typically don't care (this is a generalisation of course) and it is understandable.

If we can be more compassionate, if we see the negatives go with the positives, then we would see that even we, the younger generations, are scared or troubled by technological advances and changes, such as AI. Or how negative social media appears to have become for many people today, technology is a concern for everyone, regardless of age. To really understand this perspective, it only requires compassion towards others, in short negatives go with positives.

If in 50 years the youngest generation to us now see us 'old' people as in resistance to technological advances, it would serve as irony and perhaps self-reflection? What we ideally need to do is be more compassionate, or at least see beyond our immediate window of reference. For those who can't, the world will bring you down to reality. If we puff ourselves up, we aren't being authentic, likewise if we knock ourselves down, we aren't being authentic either. But, if we accept that what we see in others is what we ourselves can also be like, we can be more compassionate. Both the negatives and the positives go together, we aren't always happy, smiling, jolly, uplifted and brilliant. The same as we aren't always down, depressed, sad, unhappy, pig headed and stuck. We are a combination of the two, if we can accept the dualities as one whole thing that instead goes together, we will be more authentic. We will be more complete, rather than trying to run away from half of ourselves, our negative selves, if we do then we may wonder why we feel incomplete!

But for some people, the Boomer Generation isn't seen in a particularly good light, but again this isn't held by everyone, thankfully. But this view is just against the Boomer Generation as a whole, not individually.

Possibly for those who dislike like the Boomer Generation, it isn't that this dislike sits directly against a Boomer individual per se, but against their wider reaching influence. This mainly concerns our financial economy, and what that encompasses and effects within it I believe. Hopefully, I will expand upon why I choose finances as the main reason for this dislike.

Many, many factors play a role into how a situation turns out, but a boom in birth rates (which is why this generation is called the Baby Boomers) has affected our financial economy. This goes along with other factors that have positively helped many, but not all, Boomers, in a financially stabilising economy. I will try to elaborate and explain.

Again, take this as generalisations, as it is difficult to explain situations otherwise.

The Boomer Economy:

"A society grows great when old men plant trees whose shade they know they shall never sit in." This is an old Greek proverb.

This proverb seems to show true; it has indeed been the case for many people born into the Baby Boomer Generation.

'Planted trees' are the varying government incentive schemes that have rebuilt our economies following World War 2. They tremendously helped both countries, being the UK and America. These 'planted trees' have indeed helped many people, but by those who never sat beneath them. The people born within the Boomer Generation reaped what had been sown, they made use of what they had been given.

Because of this, our modern society is a much richer and wealthier place than it has even been in history! This is a fantastic thing in many ways. But, if a society that values money above all else has our society as an end result, shouldn't we all be much happier as an end result? If not, then perhaps happiness isn't found in money as the hippies were saying during the 60s? What went wrong then if a society that is rich in material wealth is so unhappy mentally? I feel that our society is in a bad way today, if we acknowledge that mental health is the worst it has ever been, young people cannot afford housing, find financial issues, gender issues and many, many more issues.

Other factors play into these results we see today, but government involvement has been a large part. The industrial revolution, the motor trade, building trade and many more trades and factors play their role in achieving today's rich economy.

So, why has a resentment developed against the Boomer Generation, for at least some people of our younger generations? If those who rebuilt, reshaped and produced such a society of wealth, technological progress and the internet, then why has all this hate towards them developed?

Well, for the Boomer Generation, they have reached a point where many of the younger generation can only even aspire to become like them in a financial way. The Greek proverb I mentioned earlier fits well here. This is not what the Boomer Generation has done for others, even though they received this in their younger age. I spoke about a potential reason why this might be in the Hippie peace symbol chapter, and what negative effect nuclear war may have had on people's psychology.

The financial abilities between Baby Boomers and the younger generations is sadly disproportionate, especially for many Americans. According to research carried out by "Consumer Affairs Research" Generation Z (those born in the mid to late 90s and up to 2012) have 86% less purchasing power in their 20s than Baby Boomers who were the same age. Again, this is disproportionate. Although wages have increased by 80% since the 1970s, the consumer price index has also increased by 500%!!! This of course negatively effects the quality of life for many young American and British people. I feel this lack in quality of life might be a guiding factor towards this dislike. Especially if younger people blame those who are older, or those who should be wiser. Many young people hold the opinion that if you create a scenario, you will have to be cynical to ridicule those who struggle because of it. I must say, I actually agree with them on this point! Accountability goes a long way.

So, how has this happened?

First, what must be considered here is perspective. Although research, fancy looking numbers and gathering data is important, for those born during each generation, they will see life and their life experiences differently. The future is difficult to see, thus cannot be viewed directly.

So, I can perhaps ask a question here to give this research and personal opinion some context;

'Would it be better to be born into a small cohort of people who are the same age as you, or a large cohort of people who are the same age as you?'

Well, traditional economic theory would suggest that a small cohort of people is actually preferable. This is because it means less competition for jobs, social program's, housing, positions in good schools, things like natural resources and more. So then, how do we fit in the Baby Boomer Generation? Despite being the largest population explosion in recent history, they are now by aggregate very wealthy. It appears to contradict this traditional economic theory.

Well, in a less traditional economic theory, one that supports a Democratic system, a system that encompasses a large cohort of people becomes surprisingly preferable.

(What is Democracy? "Of the people, by the people, for the people" Abraham Lincoln.)

This is because it gives this large cohort of people more voting power, so "power to the people" is rather fitting. This provides more power towards social issues and more flexibility on marketing.

Unsurprisingly, huge social issues that needed to change were a big part of what made up the swinging 60s. Hopefully the majority of this book so far has showcased these many social changes. So, how these changes occurred was because of this strong ability for voting power. But also, lots of protests, booze and cannabis likely helped in this power to make change also.

Naturally, when Baby Boomers were younger, they voted for things that benefitted them, as anyone else would do in such a system. Things that got voted for were things like family support, stronger social welfare, free or lower costing higher education and so on. When they got older, these voting patterns changed. Again, naturally, they started voting for things such as less business regulations, lower income tax and more domestic industry protection (this would help avoid outsourcing and global competition, it typically makes earnings much higher, so, who doesn't want that?). Another thing that helped them was to vote for residential zoning regulations (this protects housing values). Which brings me onto another thing, housing.

During the 1950s, generally, housing was a commodity. The majority of the expense in building these homes went into the building materials themselves. But today, these well built homes are as much an investment or asset as they are a place to live. Now, this can be seen as an issue or as an advantage, depending on your perspective or vantage point. Housing prices today have risen substantially higher, so are you in a good place, or a bad one?

During older age, the Boomer Generation has shifted their voting power to support things like retirement and pension benefits. Oddly in the UK, this voting power has done little to help. Many people face issues of paying more tax on their pension money, which has already been taxed. Other laws on how old people must be to retire is also changing, but going the wrong way, which is older. The government in the UK is doing their best to get money back, but from those who work and pay tax, so not that wise, unless civil war or social unrest is an end goal.

Sadly, in some cases, these voting changes can come at the expense to prior schemes that supported Boomers earlier on in life. So, younger people today won't benefit from these beneficial changes that were made by and for the Boomers. (This isn't to say that all Boomer individuals are selfish people, but the winning number of people who voted has typically fallen in favour of the Boomers).

This is a framework taken mainly from the UK and is inspired by a British politician called David Willets. He is an author of many books, one being 'The Pinch' (2019). This is where I got a wealth of knowledge that I'm using here as a reference and comparison to how things were in the 50s, 60s and 70s compared to us today. If you find this sort of thing interesting, then I do suggest you read his thought provoking book. Why I have also referenced his work, as a guide, is because I live in the UK. So, I felt it made sense to use information by people in the 'know' from the same place I live in. Although America is not the UK, I would be fairly confident that the same might be true for many American youngsters, at least financially.

David Willets is or was a conservative politician. I feel the conservative trend has shifted from being one that was between the 'rich and the poor', into one now being between the 'young and the old'. This is indeed rather thought provoking.

Of course, as we can see, this voting power has helped improve the wealth of the older generations, but that being said, it has also helped the lives of many thousands of people through social justice movements, so tit for tat as they say.

What I would also like to bring to light, that seems to have helped the Baby Boomer Generation is that they were a large cohort of people born into a small world. This is to say that they had a large ability for voting power, essentially, with very little competition to oppose their voting powers. So, more Boomers who are roughly the same age, but far, far less people who weren't. This truly meant there was less competition for most things. Again, this is mainly focusing on America and the UK here, and is a generalisation, so is ideally aimed as a useful reference point.

What was different during the 60s, but has considerably changed, is that the labour workforces were much lower amongst women. This helped the bargaining power of workers in manual labour jobs, especially between men. Domestic duties were largely taken care of by women, who by and large stayed at home. This further reduced costs of home maintenance, caretaking and childcare. Again, due to considerable social justice movements during the 60s and beyond, this has since changed our situation. I'm not leading to the idea that things should change to how they were during the 50s and 60s. But I am outlining what things have changed since the 1960s, when compared to us today, and what effect this has had on our wider demographic.

So, these higher incomes with relatively lower outgoings helped towards first time home buying. Many people would live at home with their parents, like we still do today. So, this also likely helped people buy their first time homes. One year's income may have been enough to buy a house, because of the positive change in earnings during this time period. Of course, people had to endure higher interest rates during the 1970s and 1980s, but it didn't have too much of a negative effect on housing as we may think it did. I will come back to these higher interest rates soon and explain why.

In the USA, the median house (50% of housing prices) cost roughly $82,000 during 1985. (As a note, the 80s is generally when Baby Boomers would have been old enough to buy their first time homes. This is why I'm focusing on the 1980s). So, being it was a 50% median, this was the kind of home most first time home buyers would be buying. At some point in the 80s, the interest rates were as high as 15%! Sometimes even higher, but most had it fixed in at a max of 15%. This helped to prevent housing repayments from becoming too expensive to repay.

The ratio between the income or earnings compared to the cost of housing in the US stood at roughly 3.5 during the 1980s. But again, during the 80s because of steep interest rates, it took nearly half of someone's income to repay the mortgage. It wasn't impossible, yet still wouldn't have been a walk in the park either. So, is it fair to say that housing was easier and more achievable during the 80s than it is today? Well, not necessarily.

As a side note, today in the US, this ratio between earnings and housing sits at 5.8! Rising up by 2.3 times earnings vs housing. This is comparing the 80s and us today.

In the UK, sky-high inflation spikes occurring in the 70s meant real wages had progressed to just £18,000 by 1980. A typical house cost 5 times that sitting at £92,000. The ratio between housing and income was roughly 5.5, if adjusting for inflation, which was actually higher than the US at that time, and similar to US housing today in the 21st century.

But manufacturing towards more lucrative services under Margaret Thatcher, however, it helped usher in an era of newfound prosperity. In the UK this has changed again, the cost of housing now stands at 8.8 times the average income vs housing, rising over 4 times what it was compared to the 1970s/80s. It is far above the American equivalent, so is more dire for those living in the UK today. If Boomers felt housing was out of reach for them during the 1980s, It is certainly impossible for many people today. Even though housing was an issue for Boomers during the 80s, we still have a so called "housing divide" issue today!

So, if buying a house wasn't that easy during the 80s, then how come we have this housing divide issue today? What's the catch? (What does Housing Divide mean: The distribution of housing wealth broadly reflects the regional distribution of house prices. Higher house prices lead to higher levels of housing wealth in a region, country or cohort of people).

So, returning to these higher interest rates again, as I said I would; during the 80s these rising interest rates actually helped Boomers in an odd and useful way. Saving money in an account that pays 10% or 15% interest really helps towards a savings account, thus leading onto putting down a deposit on a house. Higher interest rates helped ensure that housing repayments never got too expensive either, because repayments would have become unaffordable, thus damaging the economy. So, these high interest rates are perhaps the best advantage youngsters had during the 80s era. One for saving money, and two for preventing housing costs getting too high.

Since the 80s, these houses have become assets. What is unique about a house as an asset is that it doesn't produce anything of value. It sits on a plot of land and it can appreciate in value, or it can become an income if rented out. Yet it never 'makes' money. What is also unique about housing is that it provides someone with a place to live, so it becomes a rather unique and troubling asset.

Sadly, being that housing is such a unique asset, housing affordability can put people out onto the streets, in debt, or with poor mental well-being if affordability becomes too high.

Working in busy areas, or within built up areas such as cities, it typically pays rather well. But if most of that wage only goes into paying rent, then it becomes unrealistic. The money that is put into renting isn't likely to go into the marketplace either, it may just pay towards more investments, like further housing, this drives up housing costs even further. This isn't the only case though, the number of houses isn't in line with the amount of people needing to be housed. This is linked into the political values of a left leading ideology, 'humanitarianism' is a left wing ideal. Thus, allowing more immigration to occur is a link to this view of humanitarianism. But this creates the need for housing to become more 'valuable', thus typically it drives up the cost of living making housing more valuable in money. This is to say, more people need what was only available to a small amount of people originally. This isn't to suggest a rebellion against immigration, this is because humanitarianism exists for a reason. But perhaps more realistic evaluations towards immigration are needed? This is a raw and controversial topic, so requires compassion and empathy.

So, at the end of the day, many factors play into our given scenario we see today.

What this actually looks like for many young people is this; whilst renting becomes unrealistic, along with mortgages that become unrealistic with the cost of living, people don't move around to new places, like we used to do. This is mainly because it isn't financially viable any more, nor is it realistic. This is to say, if the cost of living after moving out of the family home outweighs the cost of earnings, then it isn't likely that young people will peruse the effort. This is another thing that I don't blame younger people for. This means that an employer misses out on a good worker, also, an employee misses out on a good job opportunity. Unfortunately, this may come across to some people as defeatist, a lack of drive or a lack in wanting to pursue a career in life. Again, this is a short sighted opinion to hold, being unable to see beyond our immediate window of reference. Kids aren't lazy, adults have just made the situation impossible. Don't blame the kids blame those responsible, or another word is accountability.

Many people don't understand or see our situation beyond our small window, or frame of reference any longer, so I hope this helps. This may drive youngsters to view those unable to see beyond their window of reference in a bad way. This is how a particular dislike occurs, but it can be repaired if people could look beyond their window of reference, I hope this book achieves that for you. Compassion, understanding and knowledge helps to make this change.

The housing market can negatively effect people's well-being, their life goals, their work opportunities, their family life and more. All issues that young people face today; housing is only one aspect of a multifaceted situation.

So, whilst the wealth of Boomers and their voting powers have helped them, the way the economy has gone, since the 60s, has negatively affected the younger generations of today. This gives ample reason for why youngsters, who are financially bound, to dislike Boomers.

So, many people will say that we are actually very different from the 60s and drive a wedge between the two generations as it separates the negativity from the present moment. I can understand why, and in some cases I really sympathise with those who don't like Boomers, when I consider some of these reasons put forwards so far. But running away from negativity is not always beneficial. I feel that what is lost is then regained in a different way. Negativity is the opposite to positivity, but they are two halves of the same pole or coin. One exists because of the other.

Our situations will change. Without wanting to be too depressing or morbid, the Boomer Generation will eventually die. Their wealth that they currently own will be passed onto the younger generation. This will likely reshape the situation from where it is now. What is lost will come back in a different way as I say. What is a negative can become a positive, if it is the same pole or coin. Change is possible, many other things in the world can also change, so, optimism and hope is still within reach. It all relies on our attitudes that we take towards these issues. What perspective do you want to hold? I will return to this change in perspective later on in this book. But for now, are you a victim of our situation? Or are you a master of your own destiny?

A final link between the 60s and us today, we are special!

In chapter one of this book, I wrote this;

"The Boomer Generation began in 1946, just after WW2 had ended. Many people either knowingly or unknowingly saw this post war era as a new beginning for humanity. People were able to see the world in a new, raw and unfiltered way. But it opened people up to the sensitivity of the situation, creating a need for social change. No longer are the down trodden of society going to be treated the way they had been in the past, especially after what had happened during these 2 world wars. After all, this was now a new era of humanity, so, let's act like it!"

In short, they felt that they were special. Now, what may surprise many of us today is that we now see and imagine ourselves in much the same way. We are a 'new era' of humanity, we are special!

We don't have 2 world wars as a back drop to our 21st century narrative, but what we do have that shook our world is something entirely different! We call our new age 'The Information Age', all because of the World Wide Web, aka; the internet and social media.

This has rocked our world and changed it beyond recognition. This is almost like having two world wars, but, in a unique, new and different way. Can you name the things that run on the internet today? I will start with the first one: Shipping. They use 'Navigation Aids', ships use a variety of navigation aids, such as radar, GPS, and electronic chart displays, this helps them navigate safely in and out of ports, most of these are connected to the internet. They also run on computer systems that log and control where items are located, what place they need to be and when by. This is only one of many, many things that runs on our information age technology. Our world would literally collapse if the internet ever went wrong, that is how much it has changed humanity, just like World War 1 and 2.

For us today, we, just like the people of the 50s and 60s now see ourselves as the dawn of a new age in history, we are special, unique and different. A song called Aquarius/Let the Sunshine In – by 5th

Dimension 1969, this was in reference to how they viewed themselves then. An entire age in history called 'Aquarius'. Traditionally, Aquarius is associated with electricity, computers, flight, democracy, freedom, humanitarianism, idealism, modernization, nervous disorders, rebellion, nonconformity, philanthropy, veracity, perseverance, humanity and irresolution. This is not that dissimilar to us today, it could be something we would have listed about us with our issues and or our technologies we have today, even though it was written during the 60s. But we see this 'Information age' as OUR age. The 60s was theirs and therefore nothing to do with us now, I hope this book has challenged this concept we hold today.

Some of us challenge, put down and frown upon those who see or stick to a time that came before our new special era. Irony keeps returning, this was a very similar attitude held by people of the Boomer Generation. To be "Square" was seen as being impossibly old fashioned, so, in a way to be 'square' is to be outside the time frame 'everyone' else is in. Yet today, youngsters see older people in much the same way, spooky? So, what's my point here? Well, this is yet another striking similarity between us today and those alive during the 60s, especially for those within the counterculture.

What happens in our era really is part of us! Everything that happens to us now is therefore special. Our times are unique and we are therefore superior in some way over the last? You know what, I agree! But are we any wiser? The Vietnam War may have had less significance if it wasn't framed from this 'special' unique position that only happened to them. This 'new' era is like saying time has started from scratch, thus history prior to our 'new era' no longer becomes relevant. We seem to view the 60s in the same way as those of the 60s didn't see past World War 2.

Are we any wiser today to stop this from happening again? Would you even know to link these connections between the 60s and us today? History is a lesson we can read that can teach us what went wrong, and if we are likely to do the same again. Are we likely to make history repeat itself?

What about today though?

Who cares, my mum says I'm special...

These are deep and striking similarities between us now and those of the mid 20th century. For me, this just profoundly links our current time with those alive after World War 2. When you see it, you can't un-see it. Perhaps you can see many more links between these two seemingly difficult to join eras of time? What have I missed?

One final thing I can add here is the Doomsday Clock.

This is taken from the website: 'Bulletin of the Atomic Scientists':

"A moment of historic danger: It is still 90 seconds to midnight.

Ominous trends continue to point the world toward global catastrophe. The war in Ukraine and the widespread and growing reliance on nuclear weapons increase the risk of nuclear escalation. China, Russia, and the United States are all spending huge sums to expand or modernize their nuclear arsenals, adding to the ever-present danger of nuclear war through mistake or miscalculation."

This is a link, a scary and depressing link to the past. During the 60s it was roughly 7 minutes to midnight, and that was then with everything going on with Vietnam. Today, it is at 90 seconds!!! Nuclear war and climate change are the main factors. So, nuclear war continues to remain an issue for both Boomers and well, everyone, even us. Ban the bomb or the CND might be returning to our media again, much like it did in the past. This again makes us similar to our past in more ways than one, another odd link.

Perhaps the counterculture of the 60s got it right the first time? CND? Peace and love? Well, they might be what we need more than ever. If not, then what do we do next? So then, this leads me to really ask... What actually is next?

I believe a lot can be learnt from those who pioneered their times during the 60s, such as Ram Dass and Alan Watts as an example. But both of these figures have now sadly passed away. Many of these stand out figures have now sadly passed away, in all honesty.

The Rolling Stones are an exception of course, I doubt they will ever die? Here's also looking at you Willie Nelson.

But these iconic people and their wisdom is now either unknown by many or is just no longer seemingly relevant. This isn't entirely the case, as trends seem to fluctuate on our various social media platforms. But their wisdom is indeed unknown by many people regardless.

A reason might be because we genuinely believe that we have moved on, we are a special 'new era', and many feel we have changed beyond the counterculture of the 1960s. As mentioned so far, the hippie sub-cultures have gained a negative light since the 60s for various reasons, again, this is ironic compared to the values we still hold today. The Boomer Generation in general is also seen in a bad light also, which is a shame. This seems to have tarnished the wisdom, for many people today, about those who came from this era of time. Do not get me wrong, rose tinted glasses towards the 60s is just as unhelpful. We need to acknowledge the good and the bad, as this will be more productive. I feel there is wisdom within those people who deserve to be mentioned still, not all aspects of the 60s was pure wisdom! I doubt people of our future will look upon us for wisdom either, but like the 60s, some people today are certainly wise.

The legacy by Alan Watts and Ram Dass is still reachable, Ram Dass and his book 'Be here now' along with many other books he wrote are still available. Be here now is a unique book to read, I wouldn't say 'book' actually fits it. So, I do recommend it! Ram Dass has many audible talks, podcasts, YouTube videos and more.

Then Alan Watts with his many audible talks and over 25 books that he wrote in his time, these are all still within reach today.

YouTube is also another great platform that can allow the user the ability to reach their work, especially if people aren't open to reading books, yes, I see the irony that I'm writing this deep within a book myself but bare with me here. YouTube is also free, so that's a bonus.

But because what happened in the 60s for us now happened many years ago, the wisdom and many traits of that era, for some of us, seems no longer relevant. The era is seen as ignorant, silly, backwards or is put down in some way. But to me, and why I feel like I relate to the

60s era so much, is because I see so much of it in today's world, I feel perhaps there is something that can be learnt or embraced, perhaps it could be used to help today's context and our issues. Negatives exist because of the positives, yes, the 60s was negative in many ways, but it wasn't entirely. Linking the negatives with the positives we arrive at a place of gratitude, either with ourselves, or with society at large.

What I feel the pioneers of the 60s found was a deep sense of self. They found this through working with meditation and exploring the nature of the self, e.g. "Who am I and what is my purpose in life?". For me, with all of these aspects mentioned throughout this book so far, the Human Potential Movement seems to mean the most to me, especially when I compare the 60s to our modern world. My belief in the Human Potential Movement is that it strives to enrich and enlighten an individual to their fullest potential. Unless someone is rather cynical, reaching our own inner potential is a true life goal for many people.

I believe that there is a philosophy that was formed during the counterculture from the 60s. To me, it centres around a journey of self discovery, understanding and our relationship with the Universe, as well as pioneering innovative ideas. So much could be learnt positively if we allow the space for both positive and negative.

Many of these mind-sets and outlooks are still relevant for our world today. But perhaps I can ask a question, the title of the next chapter says it all.

Chapter 11

What is the mind-set of the younger generation today?

There is room for improvement I believe, when I look out towards society as a whole in the West. Many people seem very unhappy, anxiety and mental well-being is in a crisis. But some people do go on meditation retreats, invest in spirituality or perhaps go into therapy. But many push themselves through a career they don't enjoy and hope that the future will fix the issues they have today, such as more money, a retirement, or a job promotion. Sadly, many people live from pay check to pay check because of this hope. These are only a few situations that play a role in the mind-sets of our younger generations.

We live as perhaps the wealthiest society ever in history. Due to this, our focus has shifted towards a productivity based model, but it has helped us achieve our current position and wealth today. We may experience a financial crisis as a society, but overall, we are far better off than we have ever been in history.

Our focus on productivity has risen in popularity over decades, at least since World War 2. While we may think that this is actually a good thing, satisfaction with life has paradoxically gone down. This is a paradox, as we have better material wealth, healthcare, longevity and quality of life, and so forth, these should be things that improve life experience overall. In reality, things like personal well-being and personal meaning, value and fulfilment have all gone down. So, something has indeed gone wrong here!?

What seems to be the real case is that while we live in a society that puts productivity above all else, it creates a life for many who feel that they have something missing, or, in some cases life just feels... empty. Now, this puts younger people and our wider society in a position that is scarce of meaning. Without a life with deep meaning, it tends to actually switch people off and lead them to become hopeless, depressed and nihilistic.

So, it is my opinion that some of the world today lives in a form of dissociation and nihilism. For those who might be unfamiliar with the term dissociation, I will try to elaborate: This is taken from the oxford dictionary;

"The action of disconnecting or separating or the state of being disconnected."

This applies to many people who disconnect from the world around them, either socially, politically, within work, or from loved ones we hold dear. Our mobile phones are a decent tool for escapism or disconnection.

I feel the part of the world that this refers to is especially true for our younger generation. This is specifically aimed towards what could be called a "Doomer Generation outlook." This term is characterised and aimed at those associated with the generation born during, or just before, the information age. (This is also known as the Third Industrial Revolution, Computer Age, Digital Age, Silicon Age, New Media Age, Internet Age, or the Digital Revolution). This information age began during the 70s, but since the internet was used by the public for the first time in 1993, we have excelled our information age.

The Doomer and the terms use itself, for some of those who know may understand that the term is falling from favour now, thankfully. But it has certainly led us towards our current situation today. The Doomer may seem like an unlikely topic or is perhaps at first glance an un-relatable aspect of our human psychology, when considering society as a whole. But I hope to share some insights as to why the Doomer outlook isn't too far off from where things have been going socially, especially for our younger generations.

The Doomer generation term arose from the younger people in internet forums, such as 4chan. This links in the information age directly with us now today, these types of internet forum have become a big part of the internet itself. A so called 'Doomer' caricature was created within the 4chan forum, Doomer is a character who arose with a mind-set, or set of philosophical views that are either pessimistic, nihilistic or apathetic. This outlook is said to be held by many, yet not all of the younger generation. Typically, it is largely regarded as a very nihilistic mind-set. Issues that are of main concern for this type of mind-set include pollution, climate change, peak oil, social disparities and more, overall, it is a sense that the world is far worse off than anyone expected. The world through this lens is therefore viewed as being doomed, but many obvious negatives make it so, apparently. These negatives can be found and are seen with many extreme disobedience parades and protests, social media itself, traditional news outlets, climate change, or with concerns found amongst these various Internet forums themselves. Overall, it could be viewed as an existential crisis worldview.

The Doomer is not gender specific though, the caricature is typically represented as a male in his 20s, but this idea isn't just aimed at males specifically. The Doomer character is just aimed to denote the younger or newer generation who struggle with real world issues, but garner a sense that the world appears doomed, hence Doomer. Not many people would identify with this cartoon character or would want to be associated with such negative details. But I feel instead many people would identify with the many views and issues the character certainly highlights.

This doomed mind-set typically leaves an individual with a sense of resignation, defeat, aimlessness and loneliness. After putting these aspects together, it leaves a typical Doomer with a deep sense of despair in life, little to no inspiration to engage in traditional pursuits and may lead a person to retract from our society in apathetic isolation. This sense of doom sits on a spectrum, so it isn't just an on/off viewpoint, some may struggle more so than others, many people will sit at different points on this spectrum. So, this mind-set is quite wide spread when all things are considered. Where would you sit on this spectrum?

The Doomer caricature is typically shared through various memes. A meme for those unfamiliar is an image, video, piece of text, or something similar, one that is typically humorous in nature, which is then copied and spread rapidly via internet users, often with slight variations each time it is shared. The Doomer caricature through these memes tends to be shown going through a day in the life of this doomed mind-set. This may be in either dead end jobs, personal romantic relationships, alienation from people, using the Internet to escape from reality and usually sees the world as disconnected. Of course, other various forms of experience can be found that express a Doomed outlook on life in general, I have only chosen a few examples.

With such a negative and nihilistic worldview and storyline, one that appears to be very relatable for most younger people, the ideals held by this character has risen its popularity within the younger modern generation. Again, I'm keen to point out that the character alone isn't what people identify with, but it is more likely the doomed viewpoints that the character possesses. For me, it is rather telling on how the modern world really feels, or sees the world around them, either for today, or for our future.

As I have mentioned before, the way the world is portrayed or is currently seen has significantly changed since the 1960s. Therefore, our ways of expression have also changed since the 60s era, the way the world is now being expressed has been put into the hands of those now living within it. A certain view towards life for some of the modern west, specifically the younger adult, appears to have formed a nihilistic sense for our here and now, or for our future. This isn't the entire younger generation, but accounts for a minority group within it. For a large majority of the remaining younger generation, most are stricken with mental health issues and problems. All issues that are indeed negative or nihilistic in nature, so even those who don't acknowledge or identify with doom itself, they are certainly affected by it.

Another cartoon caricature via 4chan who is an alternative version to the Doomer is one called Boomer. Boomer is aimed at the actual Boomer Generation, hence Boomer.

The Boomer character appears to hold a set of can do attitudes but holds them in a naive way that is ignorant to the true horrors of our modern world. This doesn't paint the picture of the Boomer Generation in a particularly forgiving light. "OK Boomer" was or still remains a saying that has been used in conjunction with these memes. 'OK Boomer' is used as a retort held against the Boomer Generation as a whole, some people have suggested that the term is ageist, I agree. The phrase first drew widespread attention due to a 2019 TikTok video that was recorded as a response to an older man. The cartoon caricature Boomer suggests the views which are held by these meme creators, and also by those who further the adaptations of the Boomer character, or share the character, they appear to view the Boomer as having no idea about our society, and are seen to be generally clueless about the true horrors that the modern world is now facing. Such views are a resistance to technological change, climate change denial, marginalization of members of minority groups, or opposition to our younger generations' values.

This appears to be a unique aspect to American culture, perhaps there is a pronounced generational divide in America currently? But this idea, form of expression and generational shaming or dislike towards the Boomer Generation isn't unheard of in other countries either, much like the UK.

The Doomer and the younger generation feel that they aren't naive in contrast to Boomer though. They feel the obvious is here in front of everyone and is there for all to see if we just look. They are very much aware of the horrors of the modern world, for both the here and now, but also for our future.

The so called Doomer grew up in or around the 1990s and the early 2000s, this is where the information age really took off, and it did so in a very short amount of time. Some of our younger generations have grown up with the internet age already in full swing. Access to the internet for many people has become much easier for the modern person. Therefore, access to all the information contained within the Internet, and social media, is getting better. A constant flow of information provides a very easy way of seeing how the world really is, it is like nothing we have ever experienced before. We are able to talk to and engage with seemingly anyone across the globe in real time, but also all the time. People can now share images, information, work stuff and videos about their personal lives, all of which is seemingly easy to access and are open to all who want to look. This is uniquely thanks to such platforms like TikTok, Facebook, YouTube and more. But with all of this information, an entire world is able to fit inside a smartphone, which in turn could then fit inside your own back pocket. This easily enables the owner to see just how ridiculous and meaningless the world seems to be, at any time, all the time. This constant flow of typically useless and meaningless information, from my perspective, has a negative effect upon one's well-being. Although the information we can gather from social media and other Internet forums isn't always doomed or useless, algorithms and personalized recommendations may tailor content to our preferences. So, if we see useless information, algorithms will likely tailor yet more of the same for us, so the cycle gets repeated. The internet also presents a wide range of information, opinions, and perspectives. So, it is important to seek out diverse sources and critically evaluate the information we encounter online to gain a well-rounded understanding of any given topic. It will make what we encounter and see appear more diverse and interesting. This is my only advise on how to deal with doom and pointless social media, hopefully this helps.

So, is life really meaningless, and is mental well-being actually getting worse then?

This rise in the use of the internet to explain, showcase and express how ridiculous and meaningless the world seems to be, for some, has fostered a fast realisation that the world really isn't all that good. There are many other factors that play into this, I will expand on these later.

Generally, because this is or has been the case for some time now, it has tinged the internet with a cynical under tone. Overall, life, the internet and social media in general feels somewhat off. Something is dark or seems to give us the impression that something is lurking in the darkness. This deep sense I believe is shared with many other people worldwide. Globally, something just feels 'off'?

Now, as mentioned, not all of the modern generation has to be this Doomer character, and many wouldn't like to hold that sort of title either, perhaps many would never have even heard of the term Doomer? But people may find various parts of the Doomer character relatable, even though they may not identify as being a Doomer itself. Existential crisis is a noticeable aspect of both the internet and the Doomer character simultaneously. For me writing about these issues, it is easier for me to have a reference point to work from and expand upon. So, I am only using this Doomer character as a reference, but it is also an aspect of our very recent past, so it cannot be discounted.

Mental health is indeed on a downward spiral, especially for young women where it is currently appalling. Men's mental health is also not that fantastic either. Many factors play into why this mental health crisis is occurring, but it is a very real psychological crisis that is hitting many young people of today; some of which we shall explore in these later chapters. For many young people, it appears to be far easier to enter into a world of fiction in contrast to the world around them that seems off. I have found that fiction itself can be created to give a sense of purpose for many people. This fiction has led people to feel the internet, or rather social media in is full of 'fake' people, or that people have fictional personas. Some people may 'fake' their lives on the internet for various reasons of course, it could be a way to seek attention, validation, material wealth or acceptance from others they want to impress. In some cases, individuals may feel pressure to present an idealised version of themselves, this could be due to either social expectations, or to fit in with a specific online community and more. This situation is aided by the availability, flexibility and anonymity of the internet itself; this makes it easier to create false personas or exaggerate aspects of one's life. I feel this 'fake' issue is linked into the need to find meaning, purpose and fulfilment in life.

The internet is not all doom and gloom though, it is actually rather similar in many ways to people's outlooks during the 60s. Let me explain; many people are seeking alternative ways to deal and cope with the world around them. As I have outlined so far, things aren't that great for young people in society today, so, I feel when people feel unseen, dismissed, misunderstood and want to fit in with society, they will seek the opposite. In a poetic way, if you are obsessed by pleasure, you'll be hurt by pain, likewise, if you are obsessed by pain, you'll be hurt by pleasure. People will want to be seen, feel heard and seek new and alternative ways to cope with these issues they find in life today. This isn't too dissimilar to the 60s era, they did exactly the same thing then with such things like Spirituality, Psychedelic drugs, music, communities that accepted their values, Civil Rights, Gay Liberation, Women's Liberation and more. Yet today on the flip side, just like the 60s, Eastern philosophies and outlooks are being taken seriously again, spiritually is another aspect that is being taken up by many for its insights and wisdom. The 60s was a time of great social unrest, so people then took to the wisdom that sounded profound, unusual, insightful and new. This is the same for us now, although the issues have changed in many ways, what hasn't is that people are still seeking wisdom to cope, people search for purpose, meaning and fulfilment.

What you may be thinking is why didn't they take up our religion during the 60s that was closer to home, instead of looking to the far East, near East or towards spirituality for guidance? A majority of the answer here lays in the hands of science (dramatic music). I feel at least part of this reliance on science can be traced back to the 60s era, and earlier. This concept of science over religion isn't a new concept in other words. I feel this view is somewhat questionable, as many religious people were also scientists as well. Such scientists that were also religious include Isaac Newton, Michael Faraday, Antoine Lavoisier, these three are an example here, the list is quite substantial in reality.

But then again, on the other hand, I want to be open and not biased: Galileo Galilei initiated modern science by dividing the world into two halves. On the one side we have the quantitative realm of science. On the other side we have the qualitative realm of subjective experience. So, in short both science and consciousness was divided into two separate halves. With most, but not all religions, consciousness itself plays an important role. But by taking consciousness out of science, it splits our world into two halves. This concept is actually explored in a book I suggest you read by Philip Goff called "Galileo's error: foundations for a new science of conciseness". This is a great book if you find this sort of thing interesting. Philip Goff is a British author, idealist philosopher, and professor at Durham University. His research focuses on philosophy of mind and also consciousness.

As you can see this disparity goes back further than the 1960s, but it was certainly pushed along by the 60s era, as I will try and elaborate upon. Many cultural shifts took place during the 60s, our religion was put down in favour of something that sounded profound, new and different. A true explosion in favour of new sounding foundations really took off, like I have mentioned before it was a 'new era' of humanity, so why not update it with new and unusual sounding ideas? Science likely played a part in this shift, many new and unusual things had been recently discovered via the sciences of the 60s, such as Quantum theory (14 December 1900), satellites (1957), robots and people who had been put onto the Moon! (1969). All huge scientific achievements in all honesty. The 70s looked no different, more in the realms of physics and technology. Firstly, Stephen Hawking developed his theories of black holes and the boundary-condition of the universe during the 70s. Biological science saw Punctuated Equilibrium, a new evolutionary theory that rejected a fundamental theory within Darwinism to redefine our understanding of how diversity occurs, Stephen Jay Gould pioneered the theory. We also have the Voyager Program, this consisted of two unmanned space launches, Voyager 1 and Voyager 2, during the summer of 1977. These two spacecraft performed close flybys of Jupiter, Saturn, Uranus, and Neptune, continuing on into interstellar space as part of the Voyager Interstellar Mission. They are still working as of 2024. But these are only a few explosions of science that were awe inspiring at the time. These have undoubtedly inspired many people towards science as the real deal or is the true 'religion' instead of 'traditional' religions or ways of exploring life.

Alan Watts was also a piece to this puzzle during the 60s era, he raised an awareness to Eastern traditions, philosophy and thought. Alan had a wonderful ability and gift to share his wisdom with many people, which was at the time 'new'. His popularity during the 60s is perhaps indicative of these cultural changes. A part of this change, that I hope I am highlighting, is that we went away from traditional religions during the 60s. Really, many other family held values were being challenged and changed at this time, old values were shaken up, renewed and were considered as 'special' for this 'New Age' of humanity during the 20th century.

During the mid 2000s though, now being a touch closer to us today than the 60s, we saw a wave of "New Atheism". This I believe was an evolution of the 60s era, when at the time people turned away from "traditional" religions. A climax of scientific discoveries, the internet itself and so many other things, these all likely made many young people feel distant from our religion. Science now appeared to be big and strong enough to take on 'God' as a contestant, at least for those outside of science. 9/11 also likely played a pivotal role in an interest in New Atheism.

Richard Dawkins is perhaps one of the most notable figures of the mid 2000s, and a component towards this "New Atheism" movement. He suggests complete abandonment of religion, wherever it came from. Dawkins is a scientist who has written many books, one of them being 'The God Delusion' (2006), so he is a vocal atheist. His 1976 book 'The selfish gene' is considered a masterpiece of scientific writing, this book no doubt has helped his influential presence. Dawkins doesn't believe in an intelligent designer and doesn't support supernatural causes in the creation of life, the universe or anything else. In his own words on the matter:

"The universe we observe has precisely the properties we should expect if there is, at bottom, no design, no purpose, no evil, no good, nothing but blind, pitiless indifference. By all means let's be open-minded, but not so open-minded that our brains drop out".

Another figure of this movement is of course Christopher Hitchens, a British and American author, journalist and educator. Sadly, he passed away in 2011, but his book from this early 2000s era was 'God Is Not Great, how religion poisons everything' (2007). Many more people can be assigned to this movement, and because this particular mind-set reaches quite far back in time, and is also linked into science, it speaks to many people today. This might be because it is seeded in our social subconscious that there is a disparity between religion and science. Materialism is a persuasive ideology, especially when combined with Atheism and our search for true meaning. Atheism doesn't have all the answers though, but it seems the most obvious choice in response to seeing science and religion as non-compatible. No God? No worries, science is the only other answer!? I can foretell a change may occur soon where religion may return to our social awareness, either in favour of traditional religions, or with other religions found throughout the world.

Many, many people are swayed towards these ideas, but not everyone, some people are quite open to question these various aspects of our society. One such figure who is open to this debate is Alex O'Connor, he is also known as Cosmic Skeptic. He is a philosopher, or at least a rather intelligent guy, but he is certainly a social media personality who takes into account Atheism. He both challenges and supports many atheistic worldviews. There are other people on the same wavelength, but I see his popularity growing rapidly, watch this space as they say. He is perhaps a decent place to dip your toes into atheism, it's pros and cons, and other aspects of science and religion.

A striking real world effect for our society as a whole is this; many people across the UK and America are choosing "none" as their choice of religion, at least so it seems that way by certain research studies that cover the past two decades. One such study was carried out by PEW Research who states this:

"In America the numbers were at 16% in 2007 and have reached 28% in 2023."

This appears to show a steady increase over the past two decades in people choosing "none" as a religious choice. Perhaps the people who have left our religion behind during the 60s and 70s have now brought up kids without religion as a foundation to the family ethos, therefore, they have no ties to choose these religions or traditions. This is only one likely outcome, but many more aspects also exist for this steady change, one being a search for true meaning in new and unusual places.

But what I feel is slightly lost to the 60s and 70s is the idea that science and religion could be combined, instead of only choosing science or religion. For me when one poses that the other side is the enemy, whichever side this is coming from, then that is the actual issue itself. If we can instead look to see a mutuality between the two, rather than build an ideology on US Vs Them, then we are more likely to see and achieve progress. An organisation built on this concept to unite both science, consciousness and in a broad sense mysticism is The

Scientific And Medical Network. They were founded in 1973. I have taken something from their website (https://scientificandmedical.net). This is in an effort to express who they are and what they stand for:

"For fifty years, the Scientific and Medical Network has been bringing together individuals – including professionals with a background in science, medicine, engineering, psychology, philosophy and complementary practices – who accept the existence of a fundamental, unifying and transcendent reality.

Given the current divisive and disconnected state of the world, we maintain that there is a pressing need for a worldview that goes beyond the prevailing materialist ethos and provides the rising generation with an orienting sense of meaning and purpose."

I am guilty of being sceptical about such groups or organisations, mainly because I, like many others, have been brought up with a mechanical or materialistic worldview. What has helped me keep myself open minded is to ask this simple question: "What is it that I dislike about it? Could I learn something new from this negative perspective?" I actually found that I did indeed have something to learn. I hope that this may be the same for you also, perhaps you could ask yourself this same question?

One of the most notable books in favour of this mutuality between science and spirituality is: The Tao of Physics: An Exploration of the Parallels Between Modern Physics and Eastern Mysticism. This is a 1975 book by physicist Fritjof Capra. This book is just one book of many that explores this concept. Of course, this is a controversial idea as you may expect, but it is being looked into more seriously today, but still remains a minority group. A search for meaning and purpose is increasingly rising in popularity, these ideas, books and organisations provide real substance to this search. If this is something you find interesting, these places are a good starting point. I will highlight further places to check out shortly.

Why I am highlighting this disparity between science and religion? Well, it likely has a negative effect on people's psychology. Let me explain; science only tells us what stuff does, it doesn't say what stuff is, or what it is like to be that thing. Science typically explains stuff as being guided by blind forces and energy, without anything 'intelligent' behind it that drives it. I feel if we really believe and buy into this, then it may seem like the world has no intrinsic purpose or point, it is just a messy place of happy, or unhappy coincidences. I feel it challenges our concept of the world around us, and if a significant meaning beyond humanity actually exists. What if it doesn't, then what next?

As I say, my point here is that this may play a role in our metal well-being. I realise that this is a rather deep topic of course, but it is something that I believe plays a part in people's psychology. I would like to ask you a question here, in order to flesh this idea out over poor mental health; "Would you rather live in world that could be considered dead, a world that only moves or occurs out of random and chance? Or would you rather live in a world that has some form of intelligence behind it that does guide it with some sort of purpose?" This doesn't have to be a religious reason of course, but it would be a 'something' a 'meaning' or a 'purpose' rather than literally nothing at all?

Whichever one you just chose was likely done so out of an emotional response; this emotional response I believe is linked into psychology.

If you feel that science must mean that things are unintelligent, then it will likely have a negative effect on your psychology. Currently, most people feel we live in random and chance, or live in a universe that could be regarded as dead. Because of this, many are guided and inspired by materialism. For me, materialism is not the only answer here, it might be more counterproductive than we think, at least as a belief system.

Thomas Nagel has argued that materialism cannot provide an adequate explanation of life because it cannot provide an adequate explanation of mind. Thomas Nagel is a widely recognised American philosopher, for those who are unfamiliar with him. Again, he is yet another person I suggest you look up, if you want to do so.

What seems so convincing in favour of this materialistic worldview is linked into our modern era. As technology rises in popularity, it becomes a major part of our daily lives, so our relationships towards these mechanical and electrical objects naturally becomes more intimate. To view the universe as a mechanical machine seems almost obvious or natural to us in such a situation, this is to say that our immediate world is full of and runs on mechanical and electrical objects. For me this drives the popularity of a mechanical or materialistic worldview. What is missing from a materialistic worldview is that it cannot account for things being organic. Consciousness for me is a very organic part of our universe, therefore materialism cannot account for its existence, Thomas Nagel suggests this when he says about mind, this 'mind' refers to 'consciousness'.

Again, many factors play into our current scenario, and many other alternatives lay out here in our world. I'm not looking at saying the world is just doomed. I would like to give some constructive ideas, places and people to look into that will help us find some answers.

Philip Goff is one alternative example, and one who I personally am sympathetic towards. He is a modern philosopher who expresses the idea that the universe isn't as un-intelligent as we may think. He sits with the idea of Panpsychism; this is a belief that suggests consciousness is a fundamental part of reality. This actually makes the universe, through a scientific lens, more 'alive' or 'intelligent', without the need for spooks, spirits, woo-woo, or religious deities. He is another person I highly suggest you look up if you want to explore this further.

I am very open to looking at something through many lenses, so I suggest also looking up Donald Hoffman, he seems to be opposed in some ways to Philip Goff and his philosophical standing. So, I hope these suggestions give some form of intellectual openness, especially when it is such a deep and philosophical matter. Donald Hoffman studies consciousness, visual perception and evolutionary psychology using mathematical models and psychophysical experiments.

What seems to be the main opposition against Panpsychism is: 'the combination problem'. Stated generally, the combination problem is the problem of how precisely the fundamental conscious minds come to compose, constitute, or give rise to some further, additional conscious mind (especially our own). So, my sympathy towards such an idea is not without fault either.

Hopefully, this gives some flexibility for thought. I don't want to only state the problem, I would also like to suggest some resolutions to these issues as well.

Summary:
So, here we are, we certainly appear to be struggling with the world today, with such things like poor mental health, and a whole host of other social changes and issues. So, I guess this is a good place to lead onto the next chapter.

Chapter 12

Are we Doomed? The issues of society and the directions we are headed.

What I feel is that the Doomer worldview and nihilism isn't overall necessarily wrong, this outlook on life is indeed riddled with doom, the world around us in a way is seemingly doomed.

But it isn't just this assessment of life being doomed that is the problem here, it is the way this view of doom is being dealt with. Therefore, I would like to take you through some ideas, concepts and ways to resolve these issues of nihilism and doom.

I want to make this chapter more uplifting, I know the last chapter was slightly depressing, so hold in there folks. We have more in life than doom.

Throughout history doom has been continually present, but here we are today. Doom hasn't killed us off and it isn't the spell of misfortune for things to happen either, I am not the first person to realise this. Pick up a history book and find something you would call "Doom". It could be torture, the plague, genocide towards native people whose country was being invaded and more. Doom or perhaps nihilism is certainly evident, so it would appear that nihilism is a preferable view to hold.

Initially, I would like to explore how this nihilistic mind-set has crept into our society today, and how it has affected us. But by doing so, it will allow us to understand and recognise the issues we now face and what to do next.

Nihilism, how can we find purpose, meaning and fulfilment?

Popular philosophy has been created in history with this doomed outlook in mind, often called Nihilism. A Nihilist would believe in nothing, have no loyalties and have a lacking sense of self purpose. I understand that there are many interpretations of what nihilism actually is or means, but this seems to be the general consensus. I would like to point out that Nihilism is a lot like the Doomer caricature.

Popular nihilistic philosophers in history have been Arthur Schopenhauer, Frederick Neichze and Søren Kierkegaard. They were all alive during the 1800s, so this philosophy goes back in time during the pre world war era, or prior to our current social justice era of the 20th and 21st century. Suggestions to feel less doomed using Nihilistic philosophy is to become engaged in creativity, to express artistically our doomed outlooks and perspectives. Things such as poetry, music and theatre are seen as worthwhile because of a shared truth when applying them with nihilism. This theory alleviates an individual from a doomed outlook, helping to create wonder and expression instead. This lessens the need to engage in otherwise seemingly pointless and meaningless activities found in life.

Ironically the Doomer character is the very expression of this theory in play found on the Internet. The characters creation, story line and use as a form of expression really captures this suggestion to feel less doomed. But for the Doomer and the many that identify, or at least relate to the character, the modern world just seems to magnify this overwhelming sense of detachment, doom, alienation and also social divide.

To find a way to actually fix these issues, we will need to explore how these issues have crept into our society. I will give nihilism a framework so we can look at how this effects our society. I will outline nihilism in four phases.

Phase 1: The death of meaning and young generation abandonment. Marking nihilisms beginning impact on our society.

Because our society is built upon productivity, which for some may look like consumerism, above all else, we have lost a deep sense of meaning outside of work, or our careers.

Many people may struggle to spend time with only themselves as a knock on effect, mainly because of this drive towards productivity. This is to say that without something other than you to give your life meaning, this leaves only you for you to give your own life meaning. Many people struggle with this concept within an absence of social stimulation, it can leave people feeling detached, uncomfortable, nihilistic, hopeless or disconnected. I feel it is also linked into our worry of negative internal dialogue, one that may spiral out of control at any given moment if uncontrolled, or unchecked. For these various reasons so far, it therefore may appear as though we are experiencing a struggle, or as if we have given up on life and our life goals, society may label this as depression, laziness, broken, nihilistic or apathetic.

Strangely, I feel that this is indeed the case for many young people today. Many young people can struggle to spend time with just themselves without any influence from an outside source, such things like social media are as an example here. As expressed, many people may even be fearful of spending time with only themselves, and thus see such ideas and pursuits as negative. So, what does all of this mean?

Well, the causes are many, but this young generation abandonment term mainly centres around an abandoned sense of self meaning and self purpose, it is a scarcity of meaning in many ways. Children growing up in such a society, one that puts huge emphasis on productivity may feel disconnected from their emotions through social influence. Going to work in a job you dislike, going home, cooking dinner, sleeping and then repeat. This cycle of the day to day can make life seem pointless.

It naturally switches off emotional responses to certain situations. A sense of purposelessness, aimlessness, depression, anxiety and a lack of meaning are likely to occur as a result. Social media can and does have this same effect on people, a one word that fits all is nihilism, this is to say a felt sense towards a loss of meaning and purpose, hence a scarcity of meaning.

This may be linked with such things like family dynamic changes. This is linked into the 60s where old traditional family values were being challenged and changed. The contraceptive pill made family life very different, thus it began to challenge our concept of family dynamics, it challenged the idea of only having sex after marriage and more. Essentially, it gave rise to women being able to enter into the mainstream workforce. But it has had negative effects, especially in biochemical changes that can and does affect a women's' felt sense of self. This particular topic is not spoken enough about in our society today, I wonder if you agree? Another social issue was that an estimated 185,000 women, most of them unmarried teenagers at the time, were coerced into having their babies adopted between 1949 and 1976. This had very negative effects on mothers, their psychology and the family circle and life in general.

Because the need for traditional family dynamics was starting to be challenged during the 60s, it makes family life rather strange for us today. In our 21st century, many home life dynamics have become distorted and have fallen apart since the 60s. Family life and how a family operates has certainly changed in a short amount of time, long standing traditions where men were the providers, and women were the caregivers are no longer true. This is certainly linked into the much needed Women's Liberation Movement of the 60s era. This has changed our long standing family dynamics, but no-one has come up with nor has the women's liberation replaced any true understanding of what to do in place of these changes in dynamics. Because of this, time flows onwards and things get worse. This is not a put down upon feminism or the women's liberation movement but is a put down on the way we deal with these issues today, I hope we can reconcile these issues. I personally feel we need to allow for a better framework for equality, and a mutuality between our female and male genders. I will try and expand upon this here.

Women's Liberation is what it was called and known as during the 60s, I have explored this earlier on in the first chapter. The Women's Liberation has evolved, developed and changed with time of course. Feminism is what we typically call it today. The 60s era was when we had the drive for equality between both women and men, either in the workplace, at home, a drive for equal pay and more. But, since the 60s, things have indeed changed over the ensuing decades. We had the 3rd wave of feminism during the 90s, this is where feminism became a fashion trend and thus became 'trendy' and commercialised. Such girl groups like The Spice Girls really pushed this ideology forwards. Then during the early 2000s feminism by all accounts dissipated. But feminism came back in full swing again in 2012, this time though it seemed to have evolved into a darker situation on the most part, it is known as 'Fourth-wave feminism'. Feminism during this time frame seemed to be centred around a framework that was actually at the expense of others, even in some cases between women themselves. Then in 2017 came the "#MeToo" campaign, it is a campaign against such things like sexual abuse, sexual harassment and rape culture. People publicised their experiences of sexual abuse or sexual harassment in an effort to make change or to raise an awareness. Then we had Covid-19 in 2019, which changed the world. After here we seem to have more emphasis on "Girl power", or Female empowerment. Typically, I see links between our drive for productivity above anything else, and feminism, thus things like "Girl Boss" are typical of this praise for productivity, economic drive and or dominance.

Sadly, in some places it has become an Us Vs Them ideology, the fourth-wave feminist movement has encapsulated an ideology that challenges traditional gender roles for men and women, which it believes are oppressive. Men therefore can be seen as the issue, they can be made out to be seen as 'useless', whilst females on the other hand can do no wrong, thus an Us Vs Them ideology. To suggest otherwise, or to suggest that genders do exist can get someone "cancelled" or has become a part of the so called "cancel culture". This is damaging to female mental well-being, as well as male mental health. The practice of "cancelling" or mass shaming often occurs on social media platforms such as Twitter (X), Instagram, Facebook and more. This damages many aspects of life and creates anxiety for many people in various areas of life, or within professional circumstances. To discuss these issues is also often feared, people may ask off camera during a podcast scenario if what is to be said is 'acceptable'. This is a troubling aspect of this cancel culture, nobody truly knows where they stand, or what can be said in an effort to resolve these issues. Hopefully it will change, or that we become more understanding towards the issues rather than run away from them, create barriers or remove people from society.

Not many people ask how this affects young men, these young men may not understand the current situation. Young men might truly believe that something benign and awful is within them, something they can do nothing about because they were born into a broken gender. A rather troubling aspect to take in when we stand back and reflect upon the current situation. But this certainly is a nihilistic inducing self belief but taken in at such a young age! Hanna Rosin's book, "The End of Men," argued that feminism had largely achieved it's aims, and that it was time to start worrying about the coming obsolescence of men, I personally agree.

I see another issue in the feminist movement today, it is an issue where women can be seen as being unable to do anything wrong, this therefore forms an unstable foundation. This is to say if any woman can do no wrong, then it forms no relatable role model for young women to look up too, admire, or aspire to be like, but it also pushes feminism far beyond equality. For some people, feminism can be seen as being rather 'extreme' in some cases, this depends on where we get our information from of course, so this will likely skew our vision of feminism. Male toxic masculinity has spilled over into the sphere of feminism also, this I believe is linked into the diminishing requirements of men amongst society. This only proves to achieve a skewed vision of what females or males are. What is the word female to mean if such a thing as a man no longer exists, or becomes of no use? Feminism itself may lose its value if 'Female' or 'Male' is no longer perceivable. Males are typically demonised in such situations to prove superiority of women above men, again an Us Vs Them idea. But this demonising of men has led us to lose sight of what is valuable and generative in male and female difference, something that is a positive within nature. Perhaps a poor concept of equality has led us to see equality itself as a bad thing today? How can we fight for equality if the word itself and it's meaning has become distorted? Equality means nothing at all when the ideology of US Vs Them is ever more substantial and present.

I agree that this topic is controversial, but this is only for those who are driven by pleasure, because those who are will be hurt by pain. It should not prevent our society from questioning and resolving these issues today, if being cancelled is the threat, it suggests a deep and troubling fault in the foundation this 4th wave of feminism is built upon. Equality means to work together, a mutuality, a collaboration, so perhaps we need a safe space to evaluate these issues that is built upon equality itself in its un-skewed and original meaning. Thankfully, this is indeed the case on social media, and my idea of the economy of meaning we find today. Social media in and of itself might be the answer to some of these issues, I believe this to be the case already!

This drive for productivity and economic dominance can lead to burnout, this can also lead to poor mental health for women. I would guess that if females aren't seen as 'doing their bit' and fighting for dominance, fighting for feminism in our productivity driven society, then females may frown upon other women for their lack of effort. This may be where a darker aspect of feminism could form. This is only a wild speculation on my part, but a potential reality should things continue on the road as they are. Why I see this as a potential speculation is because we have the male equivalent, this is to say that if males aren't 'doing their bit' and asserting dominance, then males will frown upon others for their lack of effort. For me, it isn't too wild to suggest that if we have toxic masculinity, it's therefore not unreasonable to suggest that toxic femininity may also be a 'thing'. Needless to say, toxic femininity will hurt female mental well-being, as does toxic masculinity.

What role does social media play in feminism today? One comparison that cannot be made between the 1960s and our 21st century is social media itself. This is because it basically didn't exist until the turn of the century. Social media plays a huge role in how things are now turning out regarding feminism, here we have on the one hand the world of social media, but on the other we have our outside world, which by all accounts is actually separate. What appears to be more apparent is that these two separate worlds are now becoming one. Therefore, the issues that come with one, social media, are thus spilling over into the other, normal life. This niche of social issues regarding women in all aspects of life, such as home life, social life and work life are falling into unique issues outside of social media but occur because of it. How women view men now inside and outside of social media is therefore changing, so why should women trust men outside of social media if the image that is given to them is a bad one? This is a unique and troubling aspect of our society, as more than just feminism is seeing these two worlds collide. Not all men are bad people, and nor are women, but those who could be considered as 'bad' may likely be found in places of high social interaction, like dating apps as an example. This makes social interactions difficult in both worlds, this is if we include a combination of other social issues like the rising number of people with anxiety.

This is, as you can imagine, a unique aspect of social change and issue today. So, how far reaching this actually is can only be a speculation. Perhaps compassion and empathy need to be our guiding principles with these such issues, this isn't for just women, or men, but for both. I feel that not all men are demons, bad people, or in it for the wrong reasons, so, I can only suggest being more sympathetic towards men. Men are not an exception here either, such terrible role models like Andrew Tate who encourages hatred of contempt for and prejudice against women are the demons, this is a terrible issue unto society. Men and women who follow this narrative to put down the opposite gender is the epitomisation of the 60s Us Vs Them, needless to say it is the wrong direction to travel!

These are all part of the rising mental health issues amongst women. For me, this is not exactly the liberation women started searching for in the 1960s.

Without a respectable role model, an apparent drive for hating people of the opposite sex, very poor quality mental health, and reminders of constant negativity, at least between genders, this will lead many towards aimlessness, nihilism, pointlessness, a lack of self meaning and a lack of purpose for both women and men. Nihilism appears to be very noticeable here in this area of life.

This is a generalisation of current feminism; it will be different depending on where you are and who you are. What I write in this chapter should be taken as speculation or as generalisations. I don't wish this expression and suggestion towards making humanity equal to become 'cancelled' itself.

I will highlight the most profound aspect of feminism today, which is affecting both female and male genders; when one side, regardless from where they begin starts emphasising that the opposite side is the problem, that for me is the actual issue. This emphasis is what started the Women's Liberation Movement originally. It was the issue of male dominance over women in society in general. Today, women are becoming equal in measure, this is to say the dominant force in society. This social pendulum of dominance is swinging from side to side. But again, this is a generalisation and should be treated as such.

But, during the 60s era, this social pendulum of gender dominance sat roughly in the middle. This is where both sides, female and male, were pushed towards a vision of equality. I wish to expand upon the concept of equality for a moment in a rather odd way, as our concept of gender equality has become skewed since the 60s.

Equality to me is very similar to an ancient Chinese school of thought known as Yin-Yang. This is where both sides are two equal halves of one complete whole. This seems to have been a likely ideology during the 60s, when equality was the selling point to the Women's Liberation Movement. This is because other cultural changes were also in favour of Eastern philosophy, these changes sat outside of the Women's Liberation movement, but the two managed to cross paths. In essence, equality during the 60s was much closer to the yin-yang philosophy of the far East than it is today.

But today, the pendulum has swung the opposite way in favour of women, but at the expense of men, this truly puts feminism far beyond equality. In short, equality sees both genders as equal in value, but holds a space for both and supports the difference, this is no longer the case. Because of this, it puts both genders mental health at risk, it also smells like some sort of horrible far right rebellion will occur if things remain the same.

Why mental well-being is so poor currently, for women especially, might be linked into this poor foundation. A foundation that is largely built upon an us vs them ideology. This is to say that other aspects of life that are built upon such a foundation will therefore suffer. Aspects like romantic relationships, self meaning, meaning in general, purpose, identity, work life and more will worsen. This is not to highlight any need whatsoever to push society towards a male dominated platform again, it didn't work before, it won't work again. Likewise, female dominance is also just as destructive as the male equivalent. What we need to push for is simple, we just need original equality, similar to that of the yin-yang philosophy. When two halves of an equal whole are in mutuality, then things will smooth out and become much better. I cannot emphasize this enough, neither side is the problem, anyone who suggests that one side is the problem I am afraid is actually the problem itself.

I am unable to predict the future, but I know this; If a liberation for humanity based on equality (Female and Male) is to become "cancelled" then it will drive our society into destruction, that I am sure of. If we ignore this issue we will fall apart. A very far right rebellion will soon come if things do not even out and embrace equality! This is because the issues caused by such an ideology of US Vs Them sits far outside of feminism, the influence of this ideology is very far reaching. I know that this has been a long section regarding feminism, but I feel it is rather serious upon its influence today.

Yet again to state the much needed obvious here; both men and women are equal halves to one complete whole, Nihilism here is very destructive in its power. Today, whilst this issue of feminism carries on, then men's, boys, women's and girl's mental well-being will suffer and worsen. Purpose, meaning, identity, spiritual worth and more are all part of our sphere of mental health. We need to celebrate each other for who we are, equality must be part of that celebration! I don't want to only highlight the issues here, I wish to also share some potential answers, and one is equality for humanity.

Moving away from feminism here, for many young people today, what is seen as a "flex" (something that is good or positive within one's life) is actually just being in a family that hasn't fallen apart, is loving and is still in tact. This is heart-breaking in many ways, situations like these are where the issues hit deep.

Another issue is intergenerational trauma; this is where one generation passes down the issues they had onto the next generation. This is to say the previous generation to us also grew up in a society led by productivity. This is perhaps where the forming view that confuses money between wealth was born. One becomes confused with the other, in other words money doesn't always mean wealth. Wealth is perhaps not found in many material things we own, or things we might have the potential to own, nor is it to be found in money itself. Worth is to be found in our family, personal meaning, spiritual meaning and our social and personal endeavours.

Can you answer me this; How rich are we within all of these things?

One of the final aspects of this first phase is psychology. Currently, mental health is seeing a crisis amongst young people today. The majority of researchers suggest it is currently the worst it has ever been in history. So, where to begin?

Without sufficient emotional regulation present from a caregiver or parent, at least from a young age, children can grow up with unstable emotional self regulation. Most of the issues for poor mental health for youngsters today falls on parents or caregiver's shoulders. I don't believe the children or young adults are the issue themselves.

Whilst there are some very intelligent and wonderful psychologists or counsellors, I believe it is the framework from which they work from that appears to be a potential issue. Many, many young people are labelled as having mental health problems, these labels then become identities. These identities therefore become part of that person, if it becomes a central focus, or becomes part of their identity, but is ignored by those who matter, it then makes these psychological issues difficult to heal. The rising number who use medication to deal with mental health issues is also increasing with youngsters, which is also alarming. This is only speculation and a potential reason for how, or why mental health is declining. I am sure that there are many, many reasons.

As traditional family dynamics are changing, getting worse and in many cases falling apart, this links into the psychology of young children. It questions who they can trust and who they can turn to for help. A family might be an unsuitable option to turn to If mum works, dad works, or either mum or dad no longer exist, perhaps 'family life' is not as trust worthy as it used to be. But then again, many parents are amazingly good people, so again this is a generalisation.

A therapist or counsellor is a likely person who young people now turn to for support. This just starts the cycle of mental health identity formation and the process begins. Like with parents, many therapists or counsellors are also good people, so this isn't to downplay the importance of psychotherapy. In fact, because parents or caregivers appear to be the issue, not the kids, a better understanding of mental health is needed amongst adults. Perhaps this is the leading answer for children's mental health, instead of focusing on educating only the kids, educate the parents also. Family issues are often thought of as only between adults, but what about the kids? The kids aren't alright, but they aren't the issue, this is a profound misconception. Most people confuse the two to mean the same thing, they may think the kids aren't alright, therefore the kids are the issue.

Young people tend to use psychological issues and labels as games of one-upmanship, feeling a sense of superiority for having these such issues. On the other hand, other young people may feel isolation, disparity, depression and more for having these labels. Again, I return to meaning, purpose and fulfilment for the driving reasons. These actions of one-upmanship social games can give these young people a sense of meaning in an otherwise adverse situation. Social media is a noticeable place that this appears to be happening. Many people share stories, un-licensed advice, or a day in the life of mental health issues. Mental health 'trends' on social media, this is an upsetting situation. Social media can become a place of compassion and evolution, we just need to fix the problem that sits outside of it before prior to tackling social media itself.

This is a deep and wide issue, so far it is only scratching the surface on mental well-being.

There is a valuable question we can ask ourselves that can help with mental well-being; "Are we making this decision out of love, or are we making this decision out of fear?" If our choices are mainly based in fear, then I suggest we re-assess our situation, seek advice or talk with friends. Just for inspiration, what would your life look like if you used this as a guide, ask yourself this question about your decisions being built on either love or fear, what answer will you find?

Also, if we are struggling with our situation, we could also ask ourselves; "what if a friend was to come to me with the same exact situation, what advice would I give them?" Perhaps we could be more understanding and forgiving with ourselves with this perspective, because we would know how to help this other person, we would therefore know a possible solution for ourselves, essentially, we also deserve help as well.

I do suggest looking up people who deal with these issues of psychology. One person I could suggest is Gabor Maté. He has Multiple books and can be easily found on YouTube, podcasts and more. Many social media therapists and or counsellors exist. For women there is Kati Morton on YouTube. But for guys, Dr. Scott Eilers can also be found on YouTube. I hope these help someone who really needs it.

For adults then outside of this mental well-being sphere, this productivity and drive to produce a flourishing economy is perhaps the issue. I could ask a simple question to expand upon what this might mean; "If you didn't need to go to work, or a place of employment, then what would your life look like? Would your life have any meaning if this was actually the case?" Many people might struggle to answer this question, and this is my point. We put productivity above all else, so, if this type of meaning were to disappear, then people might struggle to know what to do in life or know how to find meaning. Things like going to school would become a profound concept in this way. This is to say that if we aren't striving for a place of work at the end of school, then what is the point of school overall? If this is so, then what is school useful for? Oddly we may say that school loses its value in some way, not entirely, but it certainly has the ability to change our perspective towards it. I would personally say that school certainly is worthwhile, even if work isn't what we expect to gain after finishing it.

Our profound senses of meaning are challenged when we directly deal with our productivity focused society or framework. For me, this is alarming. Potential things like Artificial Intelligence, general Artificial Intelligence, or other things like chatGPT, they are all things that bring this lack of meaning into reality for some people.

Because this productivity and drive to perpetuate the economy has been going on for some time, our perspectives will gradually get worse, and will erode our senses of meaning, value and spiritual wealth. The younger generations are perhaps facing some of the worst life experiences we have ever faced, either mentally, spiritually or socially. This isn't entirely due to a lack of meaning in one's life, but I am sure it is a large portion of the issue.

This meaning crisis and mental health crisis for the younger generation may leave them isolated and ill prepared to deal with life's issues. I feel that this is already the case, something like simple life choices might be seen as big risks for younger people. This is possibly driven by increases in anxiety issues, or identities that are built upon the concept of anxiety or fiction, and it is also centred around family dynamic changes.

Another issue is our generational paradigm shifts in our concept towards freedom.

Boomers had pushes for freedom of values for individuals themselves, and to a larger extent other wider demographics also, such as Civil Rights, Gay Rights and the Women's Liberation Movement and more. So, more specifically a freedom of mind, body and society that is incredibly purposeful, inspiring and meaningful, this power is held onto by many left leading idealists.

Gen Z however, they now have seen, or have been exposed to these social freedoms by and large, but they don't have much access to financial freedoms. Thus, raising a family, which has value in and of itself cannot be so easily attained. But throw away items and apps that stimulate experiences are attainable and or affordable, these are driven by and large by a productivity driven framework. Perhaps consumerism plays a significant role here, this being that material 'things' have now replaced meaning, value and fulfilment in place of 'traditional' ones. So, in short, what freedoms one generation had, the other doesn't have in a different way. Both 'freedoms' at their core have value, meaning and fulfilment that can be found within them. This new freedom for attainable throw away items becomes an issue, such as new influencers on social media, mobile phones, cars and more that are all changing at an increasing rate or are things that get thrown away for the next new thing. Thus, personality types that form today are algorithmically and materialistically driven, and or, they can grow to shape a distorted attention span. These changes concerning Gen Z haven't happened 'for' them but have happened 'to' them instead, unlike the Boomer paradigm where most things happened for them. In the end, it is clear that value, meaning and fulfilment are truly important factors in whichever way our society moves or flows. I will return to this issue and how to resolve such ideals like value, meaning and fulfilment in the last chapter.

For all of these points I've raised so far, how many do you see in your daily life now, or with friends and family? This nihilism, specifically focusing on value, meaning and fulfilment is certainly wide spread. But these issues make up our situation today, where meaning in life is decreasing or is in scarcity. This is how Nihilism, or the death of meaning has become a reality in our 21st century.

Phase 2: A wider influence of nihilism, social nihilism.

The influence of postmodernism. Postmodernism, for those unfamiliar with the term, is a philosophical movement which questions, deconstructs and challenges traditional narratives and certain truths. You could call Postmodernism an umbrella term for many things. One such thing that has been mentioned, which is linked into postmodernism, is New Atheism, or Atheism. This leaves many without traditional beliefs and sources of meaning. As a knock on effect, this may also lead to a spiritual void, this is to say that a person may experience a lack of spiritual and existential meaning and fulfilment. Postmodernism really took off after World War 2 and has only gained in popularity over the ensuing decades since. Because World War 2 was over 80 years ago, we have had many generations that have occurred since then, so it is a seemingly well established movement by today's standards.

As mentioned in phase 1, the likelihood is that this issue and lack of personal meaning has been going on from generation to generation in what is known as 'intergenerational trauma'. This will likely normalise this lack of meaning in life, we may have come to a point where people don't even know to question the issue now, this is because it is becoming normalised. So, to a certain extent, our lack of true meaning and purpose has become expected for many people, so, having a lack of meaning is just normal life in other words. On the whole, this becomes wider reaching across society, as one may talk to another, if both experience a similar thing, then the experience isn't questioned any further as it appears to be normal. A lack of meaning becomes a shared value, this shared value then becomes normal. After a while, we give up asking, we no longer question it because we almost always know what the answer will be, so why bother?

This normality will get passed onto the next generation, and so on so forth. This is only going to continue unless something comes along that changes this social trend. Perhaps Artificial Intelligence might be the break we need, or as I hope to achieve with this book, to spread an awareness to these issues of society, thus prevent this nihilistic trend from occurring. When it is seen, it cannot be unseen, that is my hope.

Our social philosophy needs to change and we need to be able to find meaning, value and fulfilment. This is what I'm keen on pointing out. We need to change our view. Luckily, this is actually happening already, so I am very optimistic.

Phase 3: Science, spirituality, God and cosmology.

Well, that's a profound title, but it may not be too profound when you see what this title means or is pointing out.

Since World War 2, I have mentioned the rising popularity for postmodernism, a word that is possibly linked into our so called "post-war" era. But our post-war era has seen extreme changes in science, with such theories like Quantum mechanics, physics and more. Or, with huge social changes that have given our era the name "social justice era". Then there are many things that have challenged our concept of religion and or of God over a long period of time. So, religion faces many challenges form multiple angles.

The challenges that are put against religion, as I have mentioned in the previous chapter, have been going on for some time. But our ever growing lack in believing in a "Big God" idea has been driving our lack of support of theism. This lacking belief towards a meaningful cosmic entity, one that provides life with meaning, has led to the expectation of a cold, meaningless, empty and indifferent universe. This lack of cosmic purpose may reinforce ideas people hold to themselves that life has no intrinsic meaning, value, purpose or worth. This is linked into people's life experiences that are part of a productivity driven economy; work, eat, sleep and repeat, which is hardly a meaningful existence. It wouldn't be too much of a leap to suggest the universe overall appears to have no cosmological purpose.

This argument is of course profound and deep, with this actual issue being spoken about amongst social media platforms. Such questions like; "Does the universe actually have any meaning behind it?". Questions of this nature are popular on social media. An argument that mixes together science and religion is the so called "Fine tuning argument". The fine-tuning argument attempts to use data from contemporary physics as evidence for God's existence. The premise of the fine-tuning argument is that if a small change was to occur in any one of the cosmological constants at the Big Bang (beginning of time), then it would make the universe radically different from what it is today. But the fact it is the way we find it, and the fact that life is present, it suggests a divine being or creator is behind our universe's existence. This argument has been covered and viewed by many people on social media, perhaps because at the very core of this argument, we are on the search for deep meaning, or cosmic purpose. This fine-tuning argument reaches out to people as a potential way to answer that question. Perhaps you are swayed by this argument? For me, these cosmological constants may not have always been constant, what if they actually evolved over time? Perhaps consciousness has some reason behind this evolution? Science can only tell, what do you say?

Spirituality is of course on the rise again, and is gaining popularity, this could be as a result of traditional religions becoming less favourable. This is very similar to the 1960s where the same happened then. Many social media platforms are geared directly towards expressing and exploring the various meanings of life, the self and of death. Such content creators like "Gabi Kovalenko", "T&H – Inspiring and Motivation" and then also André Duqum with his channel "Know Thyself". There are of course many, many content creators who vary from one to the next. You might know of some yourself? All of these content creators ask deep questions about reality and philosophy. For me they are signalling that a change is indeed occurring, or our search for meaning is indeed extremely popular.

Nihilism in this context mixes social purpose, cosmological purpose and also meaning towards a wider lens.

Phase 4: Personal abandonment.

This is perhaps the worst, and most damaging aspect of nihilism.

People in an individual sense are showing signs of losing meaning, purpose and fulfilment for themselves. Due to a collection of all of these phases mentioned so far, this may lead to an individual feeling doomed, defeated, apathetic and typically nihilistic. This surrender to hopelessness will send a person on a downward spiral, often resulting in poor quality mental health. This may result in anxiety issues, low self worth and a need to over express one's identity to counter this lack of meaning.

This of course is linked to phase 3, people are on the search for meaning, which has become high on people's agenda. This interest in searching for answers becomes a popular endeavour. Some content creators may become hugely popular because of this, even if they may not know the reasons why they are so popular. Possibly why they don't know how or why they are so popular is because of these social issues becoming normalised. This normalising of social issues, or of nihilism itself was expressed in phase 2.

As an example, one of the most popular YouTube channels that explores our issues of society, how to deal with them and what might be causing them is the wonderful Chris Williamson. Now with over 2 million subscribers, our search for answers, meaning and purpose is incredibly evident. Please watch his shows, they are fascinating! Many more content creators who are delving into all manner of issues are also hugely popular on social media. Such content creators are Triggernometry, Big Think, Tom Bilyeu, The Diary Of A CEO and more. Combine the millions of people who are subscribed on each one of these channels individually and put these numbers together, it suddenly becomes quite clear what people are searching for.

So, these are the 4 phases. Much of what has been expressed is generalisations and or speculation, but ones that I hope to have given answers for as well. These phases are of course my own view on how Nihilism, a lack of meaning and our search for answers is driving our society today. I strongly feel this is linked into the 1960s, because many social changes that we see today have come from this time period. This therefore leads me onto something new, something I am seeing rising in popularity, which is our search for meaning, or as I will term it "The Economy of Meaning".

But before I get into the Economy Of Meaning, I will first outline post Nihilism, which is something rather positive. Hurrah!

Post Nihilism.

Nihilism, whilst it can give a sense of purpose, it doesn't really give a true meaning or purpose to life overall. Nihilism tends to make people isolated and weary of being controlled, with many more aspects outlined in these 4 phases I have outlined just now.

I personally don't see how Nihilism will help the Doomer generation, or any generation if I'm honest, in any useful manner.

According to Jonna Bornemark, who is an Associate Professor of Philosophy at the Centre for Studies in Practical Knowledge, Södertörn University, Sweden. She states:

"The paradox of nihilism is the choice to continue one's own life while at the same time stating that it is not worth more than any other life".

Many paradoxes of nihilism exist that counter the support for nihilism. So, I would like to be more direct here, I will outline three main paradoxes that contest nihilistic perspectives. I hope that this serves to be more positive than the story I've been portraying has been so far.

1. <u>Metaphysical nihilism.</u> This paradox arises from a logical assertion that if no concrete or abstract objects exist, even the self, then that very concept itself would be untrue because it itself exists.

This is a very logical assertion regarding nihilism, but hopefully reaches those who use logic to navigate life. It suggests that if you were to say "nothing" exists, then by you being a person, and therefore being a something, actually contradicts the original assumption. Something does indeed exist, and therefore has some element of value or meaning. 1 for us!!! 0 for Nihilism.

2. <u>Existential nihilism</u>. This appears to be the most popular out of these three. So, while objects have the capacity for purpose or meaning, there is no universal truth that guides our individual purpose.

You might recognise this as I outlined it in phase 3 of the Nihilistic phases. In short, this is linked into cosmological purpose.

Humans are compelled to make up meaning for themselves, and for others, in the absence of a universal meaning, this is in order to spare themselves from the nihilism surrounding the inevitability of death. This could be our social reason for creating such frameworks like religion. In this case, religion by itself puts its middle finger up at nihilism directly. So, Religion 1 Nihilism 0!

For some people, like me, including Alex O'Connor, we reason that death seems to be a driving force behind why people make certain choices in life, especially if people are reminded that death is an inevitability. So, being alive, or more rightfully being conscious plays a role here. So, a counter view to this form of nihilism is to say that consciousness exists, and it therefore has an underlying purpose. Thus, cosmic purpose therefore exists through consciousness.

Again, I return to Philip Goff and a book he wrote called "Why? The purpose of the universe". In this book he explores cosmology and cutting-edge philosophical research on consciousness, this is to argue for a cosmic purpose, or the idea that the universe is directed towards such goals like the emergence of life.

I highly suggest you read it, if this is something you have an interest in. Philip Goff is also on various social media platforms, one of them is "Mind chat" which is his own podcast series. Cosmic purpose 1 nihilism 0?

3. <u>Ethical, or moral nihilism.</u> This is the view that nothing is morally right or morally wrong and that morality doesn't exist. I say Boo nihilism...

I return again to Alex O'Connor; he is perhaps a guiding light on this topic. He offers many arguments on the case of morality, either for it, or against it. He talks to many other influential people across the social spectrum via his podcasts or videos. Ben Shapiro is one other such figure who is someone to take note of, not forgetting Sam Harris of course, he is yet another person just to name a few here for reference. All of these people are fantastic starting points.

This is an open debate of course and would take more time than is desirable to unpack here. I'm not even sure we have an answer for this yet.

Seriously though, would you say that morality actually exists? Have a cup of tea, you'll need it for this question. Fancy a biscuit?

Alex O'Connor certainly has many interesting viewpoints to hold and is a great starting point if you want to learn more about this subject. So, I hope these suggestions are helpful for finding answers to these such issues.

Another issue that links the 60s and this moral compass is Veganism. The 60s saw people change their diets into vegetarian ones. It was and still is seen as a healthier diet, but it also helps to save the lives of animals. Veganism is just an evolutionary tale of these 60s ideals. But Veganism has a broader and major concern towards morals and ethics, factory farming is a disaster of mortality, this is one of Veganism's mortal enemies. If morality is or isn't 'true', I still find factory farming an absolute abomination. I like to show people where things are, so, look up 'Earthling Ed' aka Ed Winters, he can be found with his books such as "This Is Vegan Propaganda" and "How To Argue With A Meat Eater (and win every time)". He is also on various social media platforms. I have found him to be very eye opening and inspirational, all whilst doing my research. Also, another person here is of course female activist Brenda Sanders who takes part in various organizations, workshops and ways to promote the vegan diet. She has started:

Thrive Baltimore – Co-founder of a community centre that offers classes & workshops that support people in living healthier, more sustainable lives.

Afro-Vegan Society – Executive Director of an organization that provides resources to people to assist them in transitioning to veganism.

Vegan SoulFest – Co-Creator of a festival that celebrates the culture and vegan living.

The Greener Kitchen – Co-Owner of a plant-based deli and food distributor.

She is a wonder for veganism, you can find her on Food & Justice w/ Brenda Sanders as a podcast series. Look these people up, it really is an eye opening view of our society, but also on morality and ethics.

So, these are the three main categories for questioning nihilism. So, I hope that these are of some help or value to you. I do suggest exploring these further if you find this sort of thing of interest. I have tried to note some places to start, so I am hopeful they help. I want to offer some answers, I don't want to just point out the issues.

The Economy of Meaning.

In short, the economy of meaning is to say that there is a growing economy all of its own, it highlights and searches for meaning, purpose and fulfilment. This economy is mostly found through social media, podcasts, videos, alternative lifestyle videos, books and more. They are all aspects of this entire economy of meaning, I am sure people make money from this also, making it more like its own economy.

Now, my intention so far has been to highlight that nihilism is perhaps not the best framework to work with. I feel there is a new paradigm shift that is coming, one that will reshape our worldviews and philosophies. This is a shift away from nihilism, and if we realise that this is the case, it will further propel our journey to meaning, purpose, fulfilment and also towards our own fullest potential, this is my personal north star, I wish to help people find meaning, value and fulfilment.

Just quickly, 'shift away from nihilism', this would make an awesome band name. Ha-ha. This is my book, I can write what I like, including terrible jokes! Thank you, I'm here this entire book...

I am hopeful that you can see so far why nihilism is not a great framework to work with?

This economy of meaning is linked into the 1960s era directly. But it has only become more pronounced since the dawn of the information age, and social media age. I will start with the 60s and why this era is even relevant; traditional worldviews that are either spiritual, personal, or economical were starting to be challenged during the 1960s. Many of these aspects reach further back in time prior to that era, but the 60s saw the most radical of changes, at least socially. These social events have only evolved and developed with time and have given us our current moment in history. These changes have been either musically, spiritually, environmentally, socially and more. This creates a foundation from which to build upon, this foundation is what we see today. So, it is just an evolutionary course from where it mostly began during that era. This is perhaps the most profound link between the cultural shifts of the 50s, 60s, 70s, their counterculture and our 21st century.

As meaning is becoming a scarce commodity, a rising trend is developing on social media, which is where a vast majority of our society spends most of it's time, I have outlined this in phase 4 of the four phases of nihilism.

One Canadian psychologist, author, and media commentator is of course Jordan Peterson. At times he has been controversial, at least to some degree, but he continues to make a positive impact on many people's lives. In short, he is very popular amongst many people. His most popular book is "12 Rules For Life." He is but one person in a multitude of persons who make positive impacts on society, provide people with meaning, purpose and fulfilment. This social push towards meaning and purpose is very positive for people, so, whilst life may appear to be doomed, nihilistic and unforgiving, it is but a show. People like Jordan Peterson and others are clearly defying this road to nihilism. Positivity is indeed something we can still find in life! Humanity 100 – Nihilism a big fat 0!

What pushes this economy of meaning concept forwards actually consists of many things. So far, the biggest negative that I've touched upon, and gone into some detail about, is the death of meaning, or rising support and sympathy towards nihilism. This extends back in time way before the 1960s, so has been a part of our society for some time now. As I mentioned earlier, postmodernism is certainly a challenge within society. So, postmodernism has done a great deal to push forward many changes in our society, it could be seen as either positive or negative at this point. How do you view postmodernism, good or bad?

Automation, or so-called artificial intelligence is another factor. This puts into question traditional job roles, but also puts into question personal life purposes and meaning. To put it simply, as I mentioned before, if you have no job role to perform, then what purpose does your life have without it? We as a society are very dependant upon job roles and frameworks to guide our lives. Without such frameworks, life for many people may not have deep purpose or meaning to it. This particular interest in meaning is incredibly high on people's agenda. For me, it is another cog in the wheel of our search for meaning. Content creators can become popular who delve into an understanding of artificial intelligence.

Social media trends. I have seen a rise in the number of influencers and content creators who are in favour of self reflection, meditation and lifestyle changes. Changes in lifestyle that oppose the typically busy and often materialistically driven kind. Such lifestyle changes as an example here are things like "Vanlife". This is a more self reflective way of living life, one that puts people directly into contact with nature, either positively or negatively. Who knows, sharing your bog roll with a bear might even liven up your life? Who wants more fulfilment than that? Pass the bog roll over... Content creators are actively searching for answers and gear their content to delve into these aspects of society directly. These changes and explorations are all done via podcasts, YouTube videos, books and other forms of social media, all of these aspects are alternative ways that people are using to counter our social norms. It is, in short, a sort of modern counterculture all of its own, just without the long hair, tie dye clothes and incense. All of these changes and our quest for meaning, for me, is an entire economy, again, this is why I've called it the economy of meaning.

I must bring back the 1960s again for a moment, and how this reflects upon our current situation. Many people found great wisdom in Eastern philosophy and meaning during the 60s period. Eastern philosophy for those in the east plays a similar role akin to what our religion does for us here in the west. As our western society delves into the rise of secularism, and sees a decline of traditional religious narratives, people often turn to science, politics, social phenomena, money, fame and material goods to help fill our growing void of meaning. What some people found during the 60s though was eastern philosophy could be deeply integrated into daily life; thus, it gave a person a sense of meaning. I feel this might be a coming necessity for our modern society. As our social media trends are forever changing, one thing is for certain, we are increasingly searching for new answers and personal meaning within life. We are indeed challenging this social norm of nihilism, perhaps if social media creators understood that nihilism is on the way out, but meaning, purpose and fulfilment is replacing it, then we may catapult our way forwards and make these changes occur sooner!

Our search for meaning.

This is where the positives really come into the picture. As our search for meaning is ever changing, and for me is becoming evident, I can see a shift in focus is occurring in our societal values and trends. Yes, we have extremists, yes, we have idiots, but that isn't all that we have, extremists are a minority group, much like the 'village idiot', yet since the dawn of the internet our village has just grown in size, thus it makes us think we have more extremists than we actually do.

People may have noticed that new perspectives are forming on social media, perspectives that I hope I've pointed out so far, they deemphasise holding strong values in economic productivity, a de-emphasis in material wealth, but on the other hand they have a positive emphasis on personal health, well-being and of course a search for meaning. This new outlook instead prioritises personal fulfilment, relationship fulfilment and positive life experience, but how to reach them with our various aspects of life, so it is fantastically motivating. This again is instead of aiming towards things like material wealth or other aspects that challenge our way of life. So, postmodernism and nihilism as I am hopefully pointing out are being critically reassessed today, social foundations like neoliberalism and suburban lifestyles are therefore part of this reassessment. For those who are unfamiliar, Neoliberalism is typically a term used to describe economic theory.

It is usually an umbrella term. Figures who could be associated with neoliberalism are politicians and policymakers such as, Margaret Thatcher, Ronald Reagan and Alan Greenspan. Economic theory is always under inspection, this is because life itself is always changing, thus, how to deal with the economics of that situation will naturally change also in politics.

Metamodernism is a new philosophy that began in our early 21st century. It is a term which represents a significant shift away from the paradigms of modernism and postmodernism, proposing an emergent and convergent understanding of reality instead. Metamodernism typically starts with a bottom up, or emergent approach. This emergent approach relies on underlying systems and structures, rather than from an outside source, such as a God. So, as a good example of this emergent property is consciousness, it could be a fundamental aspect of our reality. Such things like meaning and truth may arise from such foundational elements or bottom up approaches. Other bottom up aspects could be nature, mathematical principles, a simulation theory or again consciousness.

Summary:
There is a great deal of change occurring within our societies today. Nihilism, apathy, postmodernism, and more, they are all changing and shifting. But, this is in favour of a truly positive future!

What I feel might be an added bonus to this social change is something that can be found in the 1960s. This may seem unusual, but if you can bear with me, and perhaps tilt your perspective thirty degrees, I will try to explain what this means. In short, I feel there is a 60s philosophy, worldview and ability to expand our personal life and meaning, all done in a positive way. This philosophy may just help us today, more than we might even know.

Chapter 13

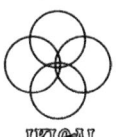

IKIGAI

Bloomer, 60s philosophy and fixing our social issues.

For me, one of the strongest standout developments of the 20th century occurred during the early 1960s. It managed to encourage many people to actualize and achieve their life goals, it also helped them navigate things like, spiritual value and worth, psychology, spirituality, our natural environment and more. Of course this is the Human Potential Movement, or HPM for short. I feel combining the HPM with all our aspects of self, spirituality, the environment, science, sociology, philosophy and political attitudes need to work in a mutuality with one another.

The HPM premise would be achieved through developing our own inner potential, and realising or actualising our highest values, but in contrast to the things that have held us back in our past. This would be very similar if I were to say to you, "We need to become masters of our potential, instead of victims of our history". Basically, if you can develop and change your own personal worldview and mindset into a positive one, then over time this will help change our wider social values and perspectives overall.

The HPM felt that people can experience a life of happiness, creativity, fulfilment and meaning. The HPM would also say that through doing so, people would direct their actions to help others realise their own inner potential, creativity and fulfilment. This idea was built and developed during the early 60s era, something I went into detail about earlier on in this book.

How does this fit in with our society in the 21st century?

As explored in the previous chapter, we are now seeing this change become a reality today. Many, many very successful people through social media are indeed spreading a positive awareness within our society, entrepreneurs and or inquisitive people are asking insightful questions about life, meaning, purpose, or place in the world and about our identity. From my perspective, perhaps this hugely growing trend to search for meaning and purpose is actually linked into the HPM framework in some way. This is to say that what we are now doing is very similar to the HPM framework, we might be unaware that this is so, perhaps no-one regularly links the past into the present in the way this book hopefully does for you?

Although the HPM was roughly established during the early 1960s, I feel it was very ahead of it's time. In today's society we are certainly heading towards a very similar framework that they originally suggested, as I've just explained. So, being in socially oriented situations will help a positive change in that person, but also towards our society overall, thus personally reaching and becoming aware on how to attain our inner potential will improve our society as a whole, in essence. Thus, the strength behind the HPM, and for it to really prosper, is where we will find a vast majority of our society, this is because the more concentrated an area of people is, the easier it would be to spread a growing awareness between them. Sadly, this wasn't the actual case during the 60s era, by default, an awareness could only spread to a minority group of people, this is because people could only contact those who were directly within reach, technology hadn't yet developed in the way it has today. They didn't have the internet or social media during the 60s, they actually had to talk to people face to face, or something rather similar, but this inevitably slows down spreading an awareness to a vast majority of people. Today on the other hand, we can certainly reach people who are nowhere near our direct scope of influence, essentially, we can reach people far outside the places we live. Therefore, this idea of spreading an awareness, finding answers and helping others is much easier and faster today. This ease of spreading an awareness has the potential to spread far and wide, so even the framework has its own potential that it can reach in and of itself. This is why I believe the HPM was ahead of it's time, ideally it is geared and set up with our current situation perfectly as we are today.

Now, as I hope to have pointed out, this is becoming a reality in our society on both sides of the Atlantic Ocean and elsewhere. A vast majority of our society today spends it's time on social media, or the internet, so this is where we will find a large network of people. An awareness to our social issues are being spoken about through podcasts, YouTube videos and more, these media creations are being received by many people who are nowhere near the place it was originally created. Now, because of this ease, I can clearly see a positive shift where people are actively searching for, and providing answers to, our social issues. This is an optimistic viewpoint to hold, but I must admit, it is coming from an almost third person perspective, one that is looking upon our situation overall. Perhaps many people don't see this optimistic viewpoint I'm highlighting, and the message many people receive is actually a bad one. The message is highlighting a world that is burning down, so, for many people we are seemingly doomed. I believe this will be translated and turned into cynicism across the internet, which I believe is already the case, I cannot blame anyone, I can only sympathise with this viewpoint, even though I do not agree with it. This cynicism and sense of doom is a picture with only half of the image on display. Doom doesn't come without innovation, healing and repair as it's very own contrast, which is an optimistic, positive and useful outlook and reality to understand. Essentially, one can only exists because of the other, innovation exists because of a need for it, typically doom, warfare or social upheaval create the need for innovation to overcome these issues. Thus, the cynicism we see and feel is just an expression of a one sided view, many people aren't able to see the mutuality here between doom and innovation, people therefore only see doom. I hope with this book to highlight this unseen mutuality, creating optimism, positivity and actual innovation in its place.

Ironically, many people are also unaware that a search for meaning is hugely and deeply popular for us as individuals, therefore many are unaware as to why they do so well as content creators, if only they knew, I hope they do now by looking and linking our past to our present. Scaling back in time in order to scale further forwards is what this is chapter in part is about. This awareness is deeply rooted in our search for meaning, purpose, fulfilment and self identity. It is highly optimistic, innovatively driven and is something I believe is worth keeping in mind with spreading an awareness. Society in a way is doomed, but that breeds change, positive change, it is something we are seeing come into fruition today!

Is the Human Potential Movement the best way forwards?

The HPM suggests that through finding and searching for our own inner potential, we are likely to spread this knowledge with others, as we have already seen it is certainly the case on social media. This trend is only growing from strength to strength, Podcasts, videos, conversations and more, they are all exposing how society feels, and what we are all searching for. To me, this trend is certainly heading in the direction of meaning, value, worth, fulfilment, identity and inner potential, I named this cultural shift the 'Economy of Meaning'.

At the end of the day, it all comes down to perspective, which one do we choose? I acknowledge the opposing view to this theory for using the HPM framework. One of the criticisms of the human potential movement has been about its tendency to overemphasize human potential for good and to underplay the evil, or dark sides of human nature. I actually agree with this criticism of the HPM, especially when I reflect upon my own life experiences. I am fascinated by searching for the mutuality's between all things in life, typically I have found that one thing exists <u>because</u> of the other. I feel in many cases we have a lot to learn from the evil or bad experiences we have in life, if not more so than the things we consider as good and positive. But if we lean too far in on either the good or the bad, one side or the other, we will end up with problems, or become unbalanced. Thus, this criticism about the HPM is not unfounded.

Leaning in on the evil or bad sides of life is also a bad and terrible idea, such things like self-limiting thinking can be the primary reason most people don't reach their fullest potential. I say this because it works in both ways, good or bad. The HPM looked upon the good and missed out the bad. But doing the opposite and only focusing on the bad is also unhelpful. In order to move forwards we need a framework that balances both aspects of positive and negative.

In an almost comical way of looking at this; 'Courage is knowing that it might hurt but doing it anyway. Stupidity is also the same thing.... this is why life is hard'.

Some people focus too hard on a one sided life, most people feel the bad experiences or situations in life all too often, and in contrast people only look towards the good and or positives. This is something I've found that most people struggle with, thus most people will run away from their negative experiences altogether. It takes courage to face the negative aspects in life, thus we avoid negativity altogether. Some people who like to put things down will call this type of courage stupidity, this only makes the negatives more negative. I much prefer the ones who say the word courage instead of the word stupid, for me life is a good show, so hurrah, life is a celebration not a put down. I do not trust those who walk around and see the world as only falling apart, and have nothing good to say about their day, or that they can't see that it has any positives within it. I believe this is my own authenticity coming through within me, because authenticity naturally searches for this balance between the two, as it does for everyone, thus overly negative people will upset our authentic balance. These overly negative people are playing a difficult, depressing and nihilistic game, mostly because they are living this one sided life built on nihilism and negativity. But, because all things are a duality of good/bad, positive/negative, night/ day and so on, they are truly a mutuality or authentic balance. But for most people, they wont see or know about this mutuality, thus if they are drawn to pleasure, they will be hurt by pain, likewise if they are drawn to pain, they will be hurt by pleasure, much like those who see and express their day with a negative narrative, they are clearly drawn to a one sided viewpoint.

So, with this view on the dualities between the negatives and the positives, I can understand why most people will be drawn to pleasure and will be less likely drawn to negativity. So, I agree with this criticism of the HPM, but in reality, it isn't a criticism of the HPM, it is actually a criticism of our human psychology and our favouritism towards positivity over negativity (generally). And, as an often unseen mutuality here, the HPM framework gets a bad light. But, with my interests in finding a mutuality between the negatives and the positives, I have found they exist because of each other, a secret conspiracy actually arises here, because if this is so, really the two sides are actually as one whole thing. If we embrace both sides and allow space for both, we will become balanced and whole. This is very similar to the yin-yang symbol, or similar to a material coin, this is because as soon as you create one side of a coin, you automatically create the other side, but each side is an equal half of the coin as a whole.

Let me explain this without using coins for a moment and lean into human psychology; If we run away from our negative experiences, we might wonder why we don't feel whole or complete. In essence this is because we are running away from half of ourselves, so, can I ask you;

are you always happy, positive, uplifted, smiling, energetic, optimistic and full of life? I can bet the answer here is no, it is certainly a no for me also. But are you always negative, nihilistic, depressed, feeling down, unhappy and miserable? Again, I can bet the answer here is also no. This is because we are generally a mixture of the two, negatives and positives are both halves to a complete person, but to balance this out we tend to be a mixture of the two. So, if we run away from literally half of this whole, we will become unbalanced, and end up feeling as if something is missing. Soon enough we feel a deep void within us has occurred out of seemingly nowhere. We might then try to fill this void with various things like money, wealth, more happiness, hedonism, material things and more. Society says there is always something 'better' in the future, so, if you become productive enough and keep working, you will fill that void, happy economy and happy person, right? Consumerism holds no favouritism for the results it gives, it exists purely to provide. The reason why we buy stuff is down to the individual themselves, but as most people are unaware of this mutuality, thus we end up with a void within us. This void is often compensated with consumerism to fill it, which isn't going to fix or heal the void in the way we think it might. This concept of better, for me, is similar to our concept of perfection, and let me tell you this; the distance between good and perfect is infinite!

I hope by explaining this mutuality between the two, you can hopefully see already how false this narrative is to fill the void actually is? What we need to do is embrace and heal the side that left us with this void originally, our authentic selves will know that the stuff we think we need is not what we actually want, want and need are two very different angles to approach something.

I will come back to this mutuality between the negatives and the positives, and what the mutuality might be saying, or what the hidden answer behind the mutuality is later on in this chapter.

Another put down aspect here with the HMP, and with spreading an awareness, is that many people might say the social media age is itself descending into madness! I partly agree here, but I will say that with any major cultural shift, for older generations especially, this shift will indeed come across as madness. This was the case for many parents during the 60s looking upon their kids turn into Hippies (crying inside). Long standing cultural traditions that are challenged may seem like a bad and terrible thing, this was certainly the case during the 1960s, people felt the Hippies were the actual issue themselves. Likewise today, the blame for our madness will likely get put upon the internet itself, or towards social media in general. But I'm not so sure that I am convinced by this perspective? This is because these issues lay outside of social media and the internet. As for the hippies in their time, it was the varying social issues that America and elsewhere had going on, it wasn't the actual hippies themselves. I hope through these recent chapters that I have helped to expand upon why I believe, regardless of whether or not social media exists, that these issues would still remain within our society. It isn't the people making the changes that are the real problem, it is the reason why they are making these changes in the first place that is the actual problem.

For an example here, let's say that social media didn't exist for a moment, just imagine what life might look like if it wasn't here (Screaming Inside). Well, if social media wasn't here, then perhaps how long these issues would take to manifest would certainly take much longer, yet the obvious to me is that these issues would still remain... regardless. Social media hasn't helped, and I'm sure it is the reason for some of our issues, so I'm not suggesting the internet or social media is all rainbows and glory. Another issue is these extremists, but since our social spectrum has shifted its centre point towards the left of our social sphere, we sit much closer to extreme left than we have ever done in history before. Thus, reaching an extreme left is more likely to occur today. Nothing much is that enticing about gluing yourself to a car bonnet on the M25 on a Sunday morning. Or within busy city centres with marches and protests, these things have lost their glory since the 60s era. But as meaning is a scarcity, gluing yourself to bonnet, or becoming involved in parades is better than nothing, and at least serves a purpose that is beyond just you, so it comes with an element of meaning and fulfilment. This is the extreme left today, at least in some of it's more socially received aspects, this extreme left is easy to reach now. But I could ask you what is more left than extreme left? Or what is more north than the North Pole? People don't really know the answer here on this topic. But when we are already sitting in the left (generally), then extreme left is more within our reach, we can only go so far left before we reach the end, in essence. The issue I believe isn't the extreme left entirely, it is more to do with the need to find meaning, purpose and fulfilment, which is linked into the HPM or our cultural shifts in favour of finding our inner potential.

So, to blame social media entirely on these issues today is perhaps short sighted, I believe if we see the internet and social media as the enemy, then it would dampen its ability to do the opposite, which is help and change our society. I see what we really need is to change our society for the better, changing our ways of life, philosophy, economic theory and most importantly our deep sense of meaning, fulfilment and potential. Our meaning, fulfilment and potential are the guiding forces that transcend time and space, you will not find life without these aspects, I don't believe this to be a controversial idea to hold, these things are that important for us.

What I hope to have shown throughout this book is that our social trends, changes and issues have been a long time in the making. I have focused on the 60s as this is when major social movements began, many of these issues we actually still feel today, yet philosophical movements like nihilism go back further than the 20th century. For example, the environment and mother nature are just as important today as they were to the Hippie of the 60s, it is only that our love for nature has become 'normalised' for the wider audience, which I believe was rather clever on the Hippies part. To be honest, perhaps the Hippies weren't as stupid as they looked? They swapped their clothes out and now look like you and me, at least after having changed the ways we live. Granted we no longer look or smell like Hippies, but we certainly act like them and share their values. So, in short, many of our ways of life, our issues, and ways to solve them have stemmed out of the 1960s era. So, I understand the HPM has its issues, there are more ways than one to fix an issue, or if you're British like me, we say "There are more ways than one to skin a cat"!? (For goodness sake, DONT try this at home kids... this is the books biggest disclaimer! Ha-ha). But what I feel the wonder of this book is, is it opens the doors for us to question, ask and discuss our situation today. The more we can break free from nihilism and a cycle where being broken is seen as a normality, we will break away from our situation overall and extinguish nihilism. I truly believe we actually can get away from this issue of our scarcity of meaning, therefore extinguish this crisis of meaning! I am more confident than ever, things are changing now today, optimism is not lost. Although many of these podcasts and YouTube videos talk about doom, and the general collapse of our society, they don't actually talk or ask themselves the fact that they themselves might be part of the answer, possibly this might change?

Now, I can also sympathise with those who dislike the 60s era as well, or dislike those who were born around the same time, namely the Boomers. I don't want to be biased, as you may expect me to be towards the 1960s. What I have said regarding the HPM is this: "We can either be the victims of history, or masters of our potential!". This means by choosing to accept the facts as they are, we might be better equipped to deal with the situations we face today. We no longer have to be the victims of the past, because the past will just prevent us from moving forwards, this is to say if we only view the past as a negative thing. Seeing the past as a bad thing in essence prevents us from being masters of our potential, and dare I say masters of our own destiny and future. Now, this may surprise most people, but if we were a part of the 60s era, collectively, we would have done exactly the same things that they did. So, when we blame and shame those from the 60s era, we would be blaming ourselves also, because we would have done exactly the same things they did, we are no different in this respect today. We now have the benefit of retrospect, which is a powerful tool, but it is useless whilst the world is burning around you and retrospect doesn't yet exist.

I know that this is an unusual viewpoint to hold and express, but I'm hopeful that you might be understanding towards it. Can I ask you a simple question; "Can you honestly say that you can see our future ahead of us? Do you truly know how the world will turn out, given our circumstances?" I know that I don't see the future if I'm honest, I can try to be wise and guess, but that is all I can do. Perhaps you feel the same way too, perhaps you can't see the future either? Now, who is to say that those alive during the 50s, 60s and 70s felt any differently? They were exactly the same as us, they also had no idea about their future either, even less so with the true reality of nuclear conflict, a similar situation that we are in today, it only takes one narcissistic idiot to end the world. This leads me to write this; we are all in the same boat today as we were back then, so, I see no sense in blaming the past for certain things, this is because we would have done the same, collectively. By blaming the past, you become the victim, then you can either see yourself as on the way or in the way of life or see the world around you as on or in the way. Are you a victim or a master? Are you on the way, or are you in the way of yourself and life? What do you choose, now you see that it is a choice?

I hope that this perspective highlights a word here that I hold dear, and that word is optimism.

Bloomer

This is where I bring in another social media caricature, in addition to the other 4chan examples I have shared so far being Doomer and Boomer, we also have another one called Bloomer. (Hurrah, the internet is weird).

Bloomer, he is a caricature who represents a person with a highly optimistic outlook on life, Bloomer has a go-getter attitude, usually in their late 20s and male. But again, like all of these internet things, they aren't gender specific nor age specific. The Bloomer is often used in contrast to Doomer; thus, Bloomer is an example of someone who has moved past an unhealthy lifestyle and depressed state. They have done so by learning to love and accept themselves, finding motivation to move past a nihilistic mind-set, finding value and purpose in self identity, self worth, the worth and value in others and a purpose in life overall. Basically, life is burning but you can see a beauty that no-one else can.

I find this sense of self love and motivation strikingly similar to what people are hoping to achieve in life today. Even if we feel that our lives seem riddled with doom, we aim to have ourselves to fall back on. For most people, this would be an absolute life goal to achieve, I know that it is for me as the author, so I sympathise with those who want to achieve this as one of their life goals. The fact many people don't have themselves to fall back on, for me, is telling on how intrusive nihilism has become up to now, as I mentioned, nihilism has become normalised or expected so therefore it has become unseen.

Our social media trends and social attitudes are indeed changing, thankfully. (Although I am a Millennial, so things like the duck song have scarred me for life, so, some things within social media will never go away). As mentioned in the previous chapter, I outlined what I called "The Economy of Meaning", I could easily see Bloomer and his mind-set here, as a person driven by life and a search for meaning, Bloomer appears to fit into this narrative of the economy of meaning, human potential and our search for meaning, purpose and fulfilment overall. I know for some, if not quite possibly many people, we wouldn't directly identify with what could be described as a cartoon character. Believe me, I can see a similarity in many ways to the things occurring in our society, but I wouldn't identify as a cartoon character called Bloomer either. This isn't to shame those who might identify as the Bloomer character, the world is yours as much as it is mine, but for roughly the other 95% of our society, they wouldn't identify with Doomer, Bloomer or Boomer cartoon characters. My aim is to use these social expressions as reference points, this is only to help explain a deep and expansive issue within our society, but in a visual, useful and constructive way to help fix a world burning down.

I would like to highlight some general shifts in our philosophical outlooks so far; we are now shifting away from this need for material wealth, nihilism, and doubt, but this is in favour of a life that is filled with meaning, purpose, optimism and fulfilment instead.

How can you help with this social change, what things can you do differently?

Firstly, what I believe we need to do is we need to find ourselves as content as possible. I'm not keen on happiness as a foundation, which may sound cruel at first, but contentment is to be satisfied with our current situation and the state of affairs we find ourselves in. So, in a poetic way to compare the difference between the two then, happiness is an emotion whilst contentment is an attitude and state of mind. Happiness is a state of emotion and through social influence it is what most people try and aim for, but contentment is a state of mind that holds a far longer lasting effect, and it allows people to reach happiness naturally, at least without trying to aim specifically for hedonism or happiness directly.

So, I hope we can realise or actualise contentment within our lives, it may just help us find meaning, purpose and fulfilment within it. You may ask "But how?" how can we achieve contentment? Well, I hope to explain how in this chapter, amongst many other insights contentment has to offer. I want to share with you a man who found contentment, but also a man that has literally brought tears to my eyes as well. He fits this perspective of acknowledging and choosing contentment over despair, defeat, loss, lack of meaning and of course nihilism, he is Victor Emil Frankl.

In his emotional book called; "Man's Search for Meaning" he highlights some fascinating aspects of human psychology typically found in soul crushing adverse situations. Victor Frankl was a WW2 Holocaust survivor and psychiatrist. After WW2 he founded logotherapy, this is a school of psychotherapy that describes the search for life's meaning as the central human motivational force. This realisation and inspiration to create such a framework came at a great cost, one that put him directly into contact with death, loss, ultimate despair in humanity and in life itself. The concentration camps he endured taught him the most valuable insights into life, meaning, purpose, identity and fulfilment. Despite the horrific conditions of such a place, he concluded that there is always a reason to live, Victor found that there is always meaning in suffering. Just like Victor, I also believe that it is not pleasure, happiness, success or power that drives people, it is finding a 'something', a purpose, a meaning to live for, but also to die for.

"The purpose to life is to give life meaning." Victor Frankl.

The first few words here are what we might think of when we tackle life purpose and meaning. This is especially true in a productively and materially driven society, a job and career are what gives life meaning, at least it is for many, but without them, then what?

Now, I cannot and will not compare the circumstances of Nazi concentration camps with modern day society. But the similarities in how we deal with adverse pointlessness and a lack of meaning in life is what I want to point out. This is to say, we walk around with similar existential questions about meaning and purpose in modern society, but we do not live in the same conditions. So, onto Victor Frankl:

When we're trapped in what Victor Frankl called the "Existential Vacuum", what awaits us is despair. During Victor's time at these Nazi concentration camps, he noticed two types of perspectives: those who had given up, and those who had not. The first group was more susceptible to diseases and death, whilst the latter was more likely to survive. The difference between the two was a sense of meaning, but more specifically the discovery of a sense of purpose to carry on in such conditions. Victor's own purpose in this situation was as a doctor who helped other inmates. He sacrificed an escape plan at one time so he could stay with his patients, this wasn't for money, power, status or freedom, no, it was for his purpose. For Victor, he didn't want to abandon these people, it was so important to him, Victor was willing to die for it. His own life had become a sacrifice of profound significance in favour of his fellow human beings, in favour of his purpose! It is heart-breaking that so much humanity could be found in such a dark, disgusting and in-human place. With so much in-humanity there is also so much humanity, what brave people, what a profound insight. This is what brings tears to my eyes with our search for meaning and purpose, despite the despair, we have hope! That is incredibly powerful! To know that we do have a choice is such a wonderful message to share.

On the darker side, the other inmates who had given up shared the same reasoning for doing so. "There's nothing anymore to expect from life". Victor wrote about one inmate who had a dream about the end of war that was soon coming, the dream also revealed to the inmate a date that the war would end: March 13th, 1945. The inmate was so full of hope because of his dream, but when March 13th passed by though, nothing happened... because this dream was naive and left the inmate without context inside such a prison, he became stricken with disappointment and despair, became ill and he died shortly afterwards of typhus. This event and this particular inmate caused Victor to question what purpose and meaning truly mean to an individual, and what it changes for a person. Looking out at the hopeless and dire situations people find themselves in, Victor asks if we can expect them to find meaning. Are some situations too overwhelming that they dissolve any hope that someone has a choice? Are some situations able to take away our ability to choose? Victor reflected upon this when the war ended, he eventually concluded that we are indeed able to preserve a "Vestige of spiritual freedom" and "Independence of mind" even during mental and physical distress. Despite all, he concluded we do indeed have a choice.

"We who lived in concentration camps can remember the men who walked through the huts comforting others, giving away their last piece of bread. They may be small in number, but they offer sufficient proof that everything can be taken away from a man but one thing: the last of the human freedoms – to choose one's attitude in any given set of circumstances, to choose one's own way." Man's Search for Meaning, Victor Frankl.

I believe that we can learn from this horror of history. The lesson is something profound, something our modern society can indeed heal and learn from. Regardless of how terrible life actually is for us, we can decide and choose what direction we go. Do we choose to live in nihilistic ideologies, damaging and destructive mind-sets or overall negative views, all because of seemingly undesirable situations? Are we choosing to become the victim of our past, present and future? Are we choosing the cold, empty darkness? What is it that we choose? What is it we would choose if we could? This attitude to life is like what I put at the beginning of this chapter, and that is contentment.

For me, I feel we have 2 choices and 1 aspect in life: In any given situation, are we 1) making the choice out of love or 2) making the choice out of fear? Do we believe that we are in a situation that happened to us, a situation that wasn't caused 'by us' but instead seemed to just happen 'to us'? If so, we may think that the situation is void of choice, but it actually isn't, it can be turned into something that happens 'by us' instead of 'to us'. This is when we can go back to the start with the first two questions: is this choice out of love or fear? It is then something that happens by us instead. I believe if we use this cycle of two questions and one aspect, we will heal our own lives in profound and life changing ways.

I have a dark story of my own where I seemingly had the choice taken away from me, I've now personally made it through three suicide situations or attempts, if that is the right way to say it, the choice of life had been taken away from myself, for myself and by myself. In the third and final attempt I put myself in a strange situation, upon reflection it was likely hallucinogenic or at least out of the ordinary, all I can say is it was a dark time, but I was in this strange third person perspective looking back at myself, in that moment I threw my own funeral for myself. This funeral allowed me to grieve my own passing for myself and enter the final stage of removing myself from this world. I believe this funeral led me to see that I do have a choice in life because I was no longer scared of death. Life was no longer broken for me because I had no actual 'life', in all honesty, I saw that I had died, so had no 'life'. Life was and still is worth more than the fear itself! I'm not sure exactly how I came to this realisation that I have a choice, I just remember being taken away by many policemen and women, perhaps it was because I could see a mutuality, but I had that choice and it was mine to make.

You see despite death, fear, loss, or darkness, we can choose, we can become our own masters instead of the victims. Bizarrely, I've now come to view it in the following way; I was addicted to death at the time, this is because I was petrified by life in contrast, but the master within me saw that the two go together, life happens because of death. I began to see that dualities exist in all areas of life, but I know for you and me, the real masters of potential, we see the mutuality between these dualities in life, I wish to help others discover this as well. This ability to link the dualities freed me from my own issues of suicide, despair, loss and hopelessness, it can also free you from the challenges of life. I was no longer the victim; I was the master. This led me onto the journey to write this book, but with this new outlook, ability and wisdom, it has led me towards a passion to help others reach their own inner potential because even despite death we have a reason, a choice and we also have hope. Life is brutal, but we are stronger! I believe in you; your potential is endless!

Victor also discovered that we have the ability to choose as well, even when life is desperate and filled with the reality of death at any given moment. I feel with this confidence in life we can instead choose to become masters, but I'm not talking about ordinary masters, no, we can choose to become the masters of our own potential, destiny and future.

"The way in which a man accepts his fate and all the suffering it entails, the way in which he takes up his cross, gives him ample opportunity – even under the most difficult circumstances – to add a deeper meaning to his life." Man's Search for Meaning, Victor Frankl.

To help us change our situation in society, the Human Potential Movement got it right in as much as we need to start with ourselves. I believe we cannot help others or fix external issues if we have a civil war going on within our minds. Our pursuits of material wealth, money, status, power, pleasure and of happiness, they are just that, pursuits. According to Victor, these pursuits are ways to cope with an existential vacuum, they are a consequence of a lack of meaning, these things are only fake cheap substitutes for what we actually value, and what truly matters. Happiness is almost seen as the ultimate goal we need to achieve or attain, some people might say it is the end goal to such ideals like Stoicism, Buddhism or Spirituality. Victor has this to say on happiness:

"One must have a reason to "be happy". Once the reason is found, however, one becomes happy automatically. As we see, a human being is not one in pursuit of happiness but rather in search of a reason to become happy. Last but not least, through actualising the potential meaning inherent and dormant in a given situation." Man's Search for Meaning, Victor Frankl.

I would say the more we dedicate ourselves to a purpose, more rightfully our own purpose in life, we will find success, but not success in a traditional sense, something far greater. Meaning is born out of purpose, and fulfilment is when we can see that our purpose or inner potential helps others, it is appreciated by others and changes the lives of others also. I can advise you not to look for happiness outright, look instead at finding contentment and purpose instead, happiness will then happen for you without trying to achieve it.

Of course, you will want to know what your specific purpose is, I asked myself the same question, this was when I was recovering at home after my third and last attempt at removing myself from this world. This space and time off work allowed me to find clarity, this then gave me a simple answer to the question of how to find your own purpose; What do you do in life that requires no effort? What TV show, hobby, interest, sport, project, idea or anything, what 'thing' do you do that requires no encouragement to engage yourself in doing it? This 'thing' is your purpose, I would even be brave enough to call it your authentic ability. Fill your life with this purpose and authentic ability, put this at the top of your priorities in life, let no one put you down for it, there is no incorrect purpose or authentic ability in my mind. I feel my own purpose is to help others find their own authenticity in their life, help them find and actualize their own inherent purpose and potential. Life is already full of nihilism as it is, now is the time to stand up and become the masters we are all able to become.

A powerful image to play with to give this perspective some space to breathe… clear your mind for a moment and look out and immerse yourself in a deep forest… look upon the many trees, branches and leaves… feel and listen to the wind rustle the forest around you. Does anything look or feel out of place here? Instinctively the answer you'll find is no, but each and every tree is different, or to use a better word the trees are 'distinct'. Yet we do not intuitively question it, we don't stop to ask if the forest around us looks out of place, or if it is disorderly in some way. In fact, to even suggest so would seem ridiculous! Laughable! We as people are exactly the same as this forest, each and every one of us is distinct but we are not out of place. Meaning and purpose are therefore distinct for just ourselves, our meaning and purpose is beautiful, but it is not out of place and nor should it be discouraged! You are as distinct as a tree, but you are as powerful and strong as the forest as well. You have that same level of power to choose your own perspective on the situations you find yourself in. To find your own reason to be alive, well, the question why should you be alive is perhaps the hardest thing you will ever do or ask yourself, it was a difficult question for me. This isn't to say that just because it was difficult for me, it won't be difficult for someone else either, our purpose will be distinct for each and every one of us, but we can choose to accept it or run away from it.

Are We Doomed?

I will tell you what I told myself after I had little to no reason to live; you are far greater in your true self than you will ever be in this fictional story you present to yourself, you are magnificent in who you are, in your highest value of potential and in your own authenticity. You can master life and make it your own! You can choose to be a pure Master of Potential! The only person to let you down or limit this ability is yourself.

Returning to Victor Frankl; by interacting with the world around us, we can find out what our purpose and meaning is. Victor himself suggests three ways we can find meaning:

1. By creating work, or by doing a deed
2. By experiencing something, or encountering someone
3. By the attitude we take to unavoidable suffering

The first of these three lays in creative work. This could be writing a book, building a project, helping others and more. They don't need to be grand or extravagant, simply sharing food with others can be all it takes. I wouldn't try to compare yourself to others and their creative work, we are distinct for a reason, thus our window of tolerance for the things we can or can't achieve is varied. What you see in the world around you, in others, and things that are separate from you, they are just projections of how you actually see yourself. So, what you like or dislike in the other is just what you like or dislike in yourself. What is you and what is external from you are as one, the duality is a mutuality which falls into all areas of life.

Let your creative work create you. What do you want from life, likewise what does life want from you? Creative work is one skill to help answer what authentic abilities we have.

The second one lays in our connections we have with other people, or with our environment. It requires love to know something or someone truly, I feel we can love a place, we can love another person in the same way as that place. Or we can love someone for the strengths we didn't know we had within ourselves. Perhaps at the end of the day, love is the ultimate reason for meaning and purpose overall?

The third one lays in finding meaning within suffering. When we cannot change a situation, we must look to change ourselves instead. This is profound and insightful, and I often find when I dislike something, or I can't change it, I ask myself this question; "is this a challenge? Or perhaps is this actually an opportunity to change? Am I making this choice out of love, or am I making it out of fear?" With this as a foundation to begin from, it can by itself change the way we encounter life. What decision do you make when faced with unavoidable suffering?

Purpose and meaning can take many forms, often it is not stagnant nor unchanging, life moves and changes all the time. We can either challenge it, swim against it, or we can choose to follow it, or flow along with this change. Ultimately, whatever we do, it is a choice! By choosing our attitude we take to life, we can turn despair into triumph! Loss into potential! Victim into Master!

By this powerful philosophy of the late Victor Frankl, one I feel I have expanded upon and also added onto with my own story, I hope to have shown that it comes down to you, essentially. You may not even know you are allowed to choose, but you can, you really can choose, hope is not lost and the potentials are endless. Upon reflection on these terrible concentration camps, and this seemingly unavoidable suffering we feel we encounter in our daily lives, I have this to write; the greatest prison you will ever live in is the prison you create within your mind.

I mentioned earlier about returning to negative and positive experiences, we could perhaps look at becoming self aware of both our positive and negative sides in life, by looking at both aspects, we might become aware of a mutuality? To do this in a useful way, we could view our negative sides in a new light.

For many people, we seem to pick out the negatives in life all too often, but this isn't anyone's fault. Through research and interest, this is due to an intrinsic part of our neurobiology; millions of years ago in early humankind, we formed something called a 'Negativity Bias', this is to say that we choose and prioritise negative experiences above positive ones, even if both are of equal value and worth in reality, outside of this bias. Unfortunately, though, because we no longer live as cavemen, this negativity bias is truly out of date. So, I have speculated upon how to actually update this ancient bias towards negativity for some time now. I feel that I finally know the answer!

I realised that both sides of good and negative actually arise mutually, this led me to believe that what we 'traditionally' call negative is actually far better described as being <u>protective</u>! Every time we do something we see as negative, look at it as doing something protective instead. This profoundly changes what negative experience actually means, or what negativity is used for. Seeing our negative experiences as actually protective it is far more relatable and much more up to date, it makes negativity more approachable this way. Thus, it profoundly changes how we can encounter the world around us, encounter ourselves and encounter others. We are less likely to run away from protection than we are from pure negativity.

What are we trying to protect? This would be our next compassionate question. This change in viewing negative as protective is perhaps the most profound and thought provoking idea I have ever had in my own struggles with life. It has profoundly changed the way I heal my own mind, body, soul and love life; I hope that it can do the same for you too.

So, what answers will you find by asking these same questions for yourself? The parts of us we don't like in ourselves are possibly coming from a place of hurt. But, when parts of our physical bodies are hurting, we naturally provide comfort, healing and protection. So, why should our emotional or psychological parts within us be treated any differently? Now, this isn't to suggest that we need to be negative people towards others, and for that to be ok, or to see this as a free pass to do bad things. Our negative/protective side is telling us something about ourselves, or telling us something about the other person, we ideally need to be mindful about what this message is telling us overall. I wanted to change the dynamics of what negative experiences are, thus make them more approachable. Another point here; what we see in the other is just a reflection of ourselves looking back, judgement arises when we dislike what we see. But it isn't because of the other person.

So, to use a scenario to help understand this slightly better: perhaps when you are sat on a train or bus with strangers around you, people you don't know, but suddenly a passenger on the opposite side suddenly catches your eye. You both look deeply into each other's eyes for a moment... you both then quickly turn away, perhaps a bout of anxiety, fear, embarrassment? Why do you turn away, is it because what you see in the other person... is you?

Because we have created an existence for ourselves that comes from a place of love, contentment and compassion, choosing who we really are is not a bad option and nor should it have to be. Don't let others put your potential, your authenticity or your own purpose down. People will bring up your past and use it against you if they are intimidated by your present.

Another aspect of self worth, and therefore meaning and value is this: if you live by your own values, you won't let yourself down. But if someone else expects you to live by their values, both you and them will feel betrayed simultaneously. This can often happen in childhood, some parents have unrealistic values they want their kids to live by, but when their child can't fulfil these values, both parent and child are let down. So, if you become stuck in living by other people's values, for whatever reason, you will remain in that state of betrayal, pretty soon that betrayal will become normalised. This then stays with you as you get older, this soon creates a deep void within you. Typically, what people do is seek validation, redemption, material objects, money, self gratification, fame and other things to fill that empty void. You may wonder who on earth you are, what your purpose is and lose a deep sense of self meaning in life. Regardless of the things you search for to fill that void, it isn't the fame or money that is actually valuable, it is your authenticity. People go insane with trying to fill a void, instead of healing it instead. Honestly, who are you if <u>you</u> don't actually exist, well in all honesty you don't exist, that void that is created is the void of you, entirely.

But your potential, purpose and authenticity is you, when your authenticity is not supported, recognised or allowed to exist, you literally lose yourself and cease to exist. Either you follow your own values, authenticity, purpose and become the master of destiny, or you go in the other direction and become the dark void of someone who no longer exists. No amount of money can pay the way to finding the self.

So, one way to start healing this void is to become that master. You can choose, analyse and identify your own values, life goals and inspirations. Pretty soon you will find meaning, purpose and fulfilment will literally come back again! You have that kind of choice; you are that powerful! I believe in you, but only if you can believe in yourself! I am the finger pointing towards the moon, you are the moon that needs to find itself again.

We might need to look at framing our ability to navigate personal meaning, value and fulfilment, so, I present to you:

The Hierarchy of Meaning and Value

In an earlier chapter I spoke about the psychological changes that were occurring during the 60s era. One such figure I spoke about was Abraham Maslow, he formed his idea called "Hierarchy of Needs" which he published in a paper during 1943. His hierarchy of needs was formulated into a pyramid shape, the bottom wider sections began with our more basic essentials. Why is Maslow's hierarchy of needs important? Well, the basis of Maslow's theory is that we are all motivated by our needs as human beings. But, if some of our most basic needs are left unmet, we may be unable to progress and meet our other needs that sit above them. This can help explain why we might feel stuck, unmotivated or lost in certain situations.

Today, I feel we might need to foster a new type of hierarchy, The Hierarchy of Meaning and Value. This would highlight different levels that are centred around meaning, value and fulfilment. This is similar to Maslow's hierarchy of needs in many ways, so it takes inspiration from his theory.

Level 1): The self. This would be initiating or searching for personal meaning, searching for what we value the most in life, things we don't need to be encouraged to do, things that we would call natural and authentic. Discovery of our inner potential and becoming a 'Master of Potential'.

Level 2): family, friend's, strangers, pets, other animals and our mental well-being.

Level 3): work life, religion, social and community involvement, hobbies, projects, health and fitness.

Level 4): Romantic relationships and deep connections with others.

This Hierarchy of Meaning and Value is perhaps more relatable for us today, our search for meaning is never ending, but, for our various cultural changes since the 60s, it has become more significant than ever. Both hierarchies of need and meaning could work in unison, mutuality, or in collaboration. I ask you this; how full is your personal hierarchy of meaning and needs? Writing stuff down I find is helpful sometimes.

Eastern philosophy

As I have explored within this book, Eastern philosophy has been a large part of the 60s era. These Eastern philosophies try to understand existence, reality, morality, ethics and the meaning and value of life. This unsurprisingly fits very neatly within our current shifts in society today, but during the 60s, with huge social upheaval, concern, disparity and chaos, Eastern philosophies became very popular. I again wouldn't be too surprised if this trend was to occur again, at least when considering our issues today, or our search for potential ways of coping with them.

The Eastern view is similar to me saying that we all came from the universe around us, we aren't actually outsiders who have been put into it. We weren't born separately from where we are in other words, so, you couldn't exist without the world around you, or things that we consider as 'other' from us as individuals. But combined together mutually, we arrive at a place of love and at a place that we call the here and now. We might say the universe is natural, and if we are mutually a part of that same universe, then we are also natural. We are the intricate details of the here and now just like the universe was at the very beginning. We are the Big Bang, the beginning, the entire universe, thus you and I are actually timeless, so, to be timeless means that you are here now.

Of course, as you may gather this expression here is inspired by the late Alan Watts. His existential quote "You are the universe experiencing itself" is rather captivating, and I do agree that what he says here is true. Alan's worldviews were built upon his love and passion for Eastern philosophy and thought, you could say his authenticity in who he was as a person existed in his passion for Eastern philosophy, religion and thought. But these certain 60s views and ideas were perhaps on the one hand a product of the era, but by all accounts, they are indeed helpful and grounding for us today. Eastern philosophy was indeed a big driving component to the 60s era, so, whilst the 60s was tinged with social upheaval, it was also a time of great innovation. I won't tell you what guru to listen too, or what meditation practice you should follow, I won't even tell you to listen to Alan Watts unless you wanted too, but what I will suggest is that Eastern philosophy shares the idea that meaning can be found in everyday life. Eastern thought supports seeing the world through a different everyday lens, I have found wisdom in Eastern philosophy on my own path towards healing, so I speak from a level of minor experience, but I am not a professional.

One helpful idea is Kintsugi (Japanese: 金継ぎ), meaning the art of joining broken pottery with gold, just as one example of this different lens. This has the effect of highlighting the broken parts of the pottery, making the viewer appreciate it's imperfections. Of course, Wabi-sabi is linked to Kintsugi. Wabi-sabi; nothing lasts, nothing is finished, nothing is therefore perfect and here lies its beauty. In essence, Wabi-sabi (Japanese: 侘び寂び) gives us a way to frame the many challenges we face, this allows us to find strength and beauty in the process of healing and repair. Many incredible insights can be found in Eastern philosophy, perhaps you can find some of personal value, or know of some yourself? For me, the insight this has given me is this; the distance between good and perfect is infinite. We will be on the road to achieving perfection without end, but the imperfections we have ourselves, they are the 'good' things that provide us with something that perfection can never reach or achieve. Another helpful idea is ikigai (Japanese: 生き甲斐) 'a reason for being.' This concept was first introduced to the West during the 1960s. It was popularised by Japanese psychiatrist and academic Mieko Kamiya in her 1966 book, "on the meaning of life" (生きがいについて, ikigai ni tsuite). The book has not yet been translated into English. During the 60s, 70s and 80s, ikigai was associated towards either the betterment of society ("subordinating one's own desires to others") or improvement of oneself ("following one's own path"). I personally see this being linked into the Human Potential Movement of the 60s, but a direct link is difficult to find. Ikigai is also linked into my own philosophy of having a sense of purpose in life, as well as being motivated. Look up these fascinating Eastern ideas, they will change your life.

I understand the East is facing its own issues and upheavals, but this shouldn't be a reason to scrap the entire idea. For me, all cultures have their issues. Today, our modern culture in the West may indeed benefit from the wisdom that can be found from humanity overall, regardless of where this wisdom originates from. The West and our use of nihilism is not helping us to move forwards, or deal with our issues. Perhaps to become open minded with humanity overall is where our progress can be found? Everyone is human, regardless of ethnicity, background or social standing, may we simply begin to treat humanity with a human touch.

The coming end?

So, as a final alternative idea for helping our society as a whole; perhaps a new business model emphasising meaning making and personal fulfilment might be where we need to go? This mixes the day-to-day with finding meaning and purpose. Perhaps an entire career or business aimed specifically at helping others find their own authenticity, meaning, purpose, value and identity is another whole idea? Who knows? With AI or AGI becoming a possibility in the future, this may remove traditional job roles in various aspects of the career spectrum? The idea of building a business model for people in this way, could be what we need today, at least in order to help others of our future and of today. This links into the Greek proverb; "A society grows great when old men plant trees whose shade they know they shall never sit in."

But the ideas, potentials and possibilities are actually endless when we find out what our purpose is in life. What could be seen as a catastrophe might turn out to be a hidden potential, it comes down to choice, but also comes down to perspective and how we view our current situation.

The way I see things today is this; if we try to be better than anything, or feel as if being better and waiting to be happy is the real goal in life, then what will happen is we wait for a future that will not arrive. As I wrote earlier, the distance between good and perfect is infinite, so, becoming better is just like trying to reach or achieve perfection.

I must say, time runs faster than you can, but we don't have to run! If we can see ourselves as part of the universe itself, we no longer feel as if we are a separate person put on the universe. If we are made from the universe we are in, then we are a part of it, thus how can we run towards something that is already us? You can run, run and run from yourself, but you will find you keep on following yourself. You cannot escape you, and the universe is you, because you came from it, not into it, you cannot run towards or away from something that is already you.

We really are a part of the universe in a timeless sense without the need to run after it, we can admire the present, because we are actually the present. Our concept of the future may lead us to think that something better is within it that needs to be attained, perhaps a better car, job, partner, house, book, or even lifestyle, but 'better' is an illusion. It is the illusion to have or to be 'better' than ourselves. But can I ask you? Who are you trying to be better than? This is to say that if your life is your own, then what better you is better than you? You are just comparing yourself with yourself which makes no sense. This isn't to downplay self improvement, but this isn't what most people are searching for in future and better. This illusion to be better means that we need stuff external from us to make us better. These external 'things' are not us in our reality. To be better will lead you to think that you need to be happy in some way, or that the future is more important than the present, this is because only in the future will you find your happiness or find yourself. But because we are the present, we are us now, we are ourselves in this very moment we call now.

Most people will run away from negativity, but towards happiness in contrast, people identify themselves as being happy, or with happiness directly. Negative experiences are feared, or at the very least are things that need to be avoided. But when they reach this better happier state, we feel cheated, or feel that something is missing; this is because we are actually running away from the thing that will make us whole, which is negative experiences. So, positive exists because of the negative, the two are secretly as one all along.

At the beginning of this chapter, I wrote something along the lines of; contentment is an attitude and state of mind, whilst happiness is a feeling. Feelings can and do pass, but contentment will last. The present has no 'time' just like contentment, so, allowing more contentment in your life can be more fulfilling than striving for only happiness, or chasing after the future and material wealth. Negative experiences are one half of the whole, positive experiences are the other, but combined mutually we arrive at a place of love, authenticity and a place we call the now. If we find ourselves running after something, that 'something' is a concept, it is the concept you present to yourself about the things you feel you lack. Positive and negative are two opposites that go together, if we feel we lack in something, we will gravitate our actions towards the things we feel we lack or don't have. The things we have I feel will make us gravitate towards the things we don't have, and visa versa. But and this is a big one I think, the more you pursue the things you feel you lack, it will only reinforce the fact that you lack them in the first place. So, let's say the more you pursue being rich, the more poor and unworthy you feel and become, regardless of how much money you actually make. Or the more desperately you want to be happy and loved, the lonelier and more afraid you become, regardless of those who surround you. So, bringing this back to positive and negative; wanting positive experiences is a negative experience, but accepting the negative experience is actually a positive experience, this is where we find contentment. We also find authenticity, which in and of itself is the ability to balance the two, and to see that the two are actually as one. We naturally find this balance without everyday conscious thought, but if we can be self aware of this balance, bring it into conscious awareness, we will become far more organic this way and more likely to navigate life much easier.

Alan Watts spoke about a Chinese Taoist philosophy called Wú wei, the English translation is misleading, it usually translates into 'doing nothing', but it is more ideal to say 'not interfering with the course of events', or not acting against the grain. Going with the flow of things is the best way of translating Wú wei in all honesty. This is linked into this idea of balancing the organic interplay of positive and negative experiences. I find there is fantastic wisdom in this idea of Wú wei for our ordinary everyday life, as explained by the late Alan Watts. So, I feel we can find wisdom from the past, but finding links from the past into the present can be enlightening also. Hopefully we have made some useful links between the 60s and our 21st century within this book.

Today, being consciously aware that there is both pain and suffering in the world, just like the Bloomer character does, but to see that there is still purpose in it all, this mutuality between seemingly two opposites is authenticity itself! Regardless of how absurd the world really is, it is still worth experiencing none the less. This sense of meaning and purpose starts with you, believe me, you are indeed a master of your own potential, destiny and future, you have the choice to choose it! In a strange way, these difficulties and mysteries we find in life aren't problems that need to be solved, they are just experiences that need to be lived.

There are many links to our modern world and the 1960s era, I hope that by starting in the 60s, we could link our 21st century together with it, and see how that what we have today is what we had then. Perhaps after starting with this perspective, you might see many more links between the two that I haven't even mentioned in this book! But essentially the biggest link between the counterculture of the 60s and our modern 21st century is that both eras are searching for meaning, purpose and fulfilment. Today, we can reach our own potential, just like the framework of the Human Potential Movement of the 60s suggests, yet in a way we are already following that framework, so, you may as well join in and become a master of potential yourself. Finding who you are is to begin with asking yourself; what things in my life do I enjoy doing, love doing and need no encouragement to be involved with. You can ask yourself how you can get wonderfully paid for doing these things, what actions can I do today to make it happen, what worked or didn't work today, thus how can I do it more efficiently and effectively tomorrow, finally how did what I did today get me one step closer? Fantastic ideas to get started.

I wanted to finish here on a positive note. So, thank you for reading my book. I hope you have managed to pick up a few ideas along the way, or even learn something new. Society really is changing at the moment, I wanted to highlight some of the most profound reasons behind why this is. It really did start during the 60s, so now you've read this book, these links between the 60s and today, well, they may be difficult to ignore!

Many social issues are prevalent today, this is becoming evident, but with insight, wonder, contentment and choice, we can make the changes we all need to see happen. This is the end in a way, but only the end of this book. So, this books end can actually be your own beginning. Social media can be used to propel our ability to seek, find and actualize our own inner potential, essentially you have the choice to choose this as your own path. "Is peace an illusion" this is what the book description asked, I think I will let you be the judge of that...

To end this book properly, all I can say is... Thank You!

A final song here for the end of this book, and a summary of the final chapter overall:

"Touch of Grey" – The Grateful Dead

Acknowledgements

Adela Austin
Alice Mcquaid
Paul Mcquaid
Callum Mcquaid
Lynda Maunder
Logan Jarmain
Izabella Jarmain
Philip Goff
Alex O'Connor
Chris Williamson
Natalie Plange
Christina Paraskevopoulou

<u>Adela Austin</u>, I have to start with you here. What an important role you have made with positively challenging my own world views, and evolving my understanding towards the 1960s era. The help and support you have given me is incredible. Your knowledge on the psychological aspects of either society, or on an individual case, unmatched! Love you to the end of the world. What an incredible insight and skill you have to change oneself from Victim into Master! Thank you!

Alice Mcquaid, Mum! It seems rather professional to call you by your 'official' name, but here we are. Thank you for all of your support throughout the years, it melts my heart to know I am lucky enough to have you in my life! What a wonder you are to the world, your love is never ending. I would not be here today without you. Thank you!

Paul Mcquaid, I wouldn't be here today without you, your knowledge, understanding and dedication to persevere is like nothing I have ever seen in anyone else. I have become strong enough to challenge my own issues, but to take them on with the same perseverance you have. I literally wouldn't be here without you. Thank you!

Callum Mcquaid, my brother! Through and through you have shown me to be who you are, and stick to that power! I see you as someone who needs no encouragement to do what you do. That is inspirational, and is a large influence on what my own philosophy stands for. I will love you to the end of time. Thank you!

Lynda Maunder, grandma. Always be grandma, who's kidding! Ha-ha, I will always be proud to be your "hippie" grandson. I guess it was always inevitable I would write such a book as this. But, just like Callum you live by who you are, and that puts you into places many could only dream of achieving. You are an inspiration to my life, and I will love you forever. Thank you!

Logan Jarmain, my son, "Little man". Although you are only 8 at the time of me writing this book, you are my superhero! I hope when you read this when you are older, I am proud of you! So Proud! Life can be a disaster at times, but disaster brings change, and typically it is a positive change. I will love you always! Hopefully we will still go camping when you are older, just to escape the world for a while, and delve back into normality. Thank you!

Acknowledgements

Izabella Jarmain, my little princess, you are only 5 when I wrote this! But, like your mum, you are as strong as an Ox, as they say. You are the most determined person I know, and yet so small! You have given me tears of joy, love, compassion and happiness. What a wonder you are, my little universe. I am so proud of you too, without question! Love you to the moon and back. Thank you!

Philip Goff, what an inspiration your work has been. I have found it fascinating to join you on your journey of perseverance towards an unusual understanding towards life, consciousness and the universe. With an emergent approach to science, it has positively helped me understand my place within this crazy world. I hope you carry on spreading an uplifting idea towards what it means to be human. Thank you!

Alex O'Connor, the master of modern philosophy! What can I say. Within a culture of secularism, your insights and open criticism have helped me to constructively challenge my views towards our 'traditional' religion. Even with morals and ethics, your authenticity shines through with a keen eye on rationality. I hope people find you through reading this book, you certainly deserve to be noticed. Thank you!

Chris Williamson, damn! You are fast becoming a popular social critique, but an entire body of information, insight, wonder, and power towards self improvement! Mental well-being is so important to our social environment, you do amazing work to both challenge and support it. You are not just a messenger, you embody the message itself. Fantastic work, fantastic person. You are the Master of Potential and Destiny itself. Thank you!

Natalie Plange, a fabulous editor! What an absolute wonder you have been in shaping what I have written. I cannot recommend you enough! This book says thank you, as much as I am saying thank you! With challenges such as dyslexia, I am eternally grateful! This is a link to her LinkedIn:
https://www.linkedin.com/in/natalie-plange?utm_source=share&utm_campaign=share_via&utm_content=profile&utm_medium=android_app

Christina Paraskevopoulou, such a jolly and uplifting designer! FABULOUS! Bringing hope and wonder towards this books creation. Thank you for your patience, understanding and dedication to create the art that is the book cover. Also thank you for your jolly and happy conversations towards the book covers creation. This is a link to her work called Book Design Stars: https://www.facebook.com/bookdesignstars

Bibliography

Allen Ginsberg: "Howl" (Book) 1956

Jack Kerouac: "On the road" (Book) 1957

William s Burroughs: "Naked Lunch" (Book) 1959

Virginia McKenna: "The life in my years"(Book) 2009

Helen Gurley Brown: "Cosmopolitan" (magazine) 1960s

Juliet Mitchell: "Women, the longest revolution" (article in the "New Left Review") 1966

Julie Mitchell: "Psychoanalysis and Feminism: Freud, Reich, Laing and women"(Book) 1974

Sheila Rowbotham: "Women's Liberation and the new politics" (Pamphlet) 1969

Sheila Rowbotham: "Women, Resistance and Revolution" (Book) 1972

Sheila Rowbotham: "Hidden from History" (Book) 1973

Gloria Steinem: "Ms" (magazine) 1960s

Gloria Steinem: "After Black Power, Women's Liberation" (Article) 1969

Betty Friedan: "Feminine Mystique" (Book) 1963

John Howard Griffin: "Black Like Me" (Book) 1961

Martin Luther King Jr: "Where do we go from here; chaos or community?" (Book) 1967

Malcom X with Alex Haley: "The Autobiography of Malcom X" (Book) 1965

Martha Shelly:

"Stepin' Fetchit Woman" (Vol. 1, No. 1)

"More Radical Than Thou" (Vol. 1, No. 2)

"The Young Lords" (Vol. 1, No. 3)

"Gay Youth Liberation" (Vol. 1, No. 4)

"Gays Riot Again! Remember Stonewall!" (Vol. 1, No. 5)

"Let a Hundred Flowers Bloom" (Vol. 1, No. 5) – Co-authored by Bernard Lewis

"Subversion in the Women's Movement: What is to be Done?" (Vol. 1, Issue 7)

"Power… and the People!" (Vol. 2, No. 7b)

(Articles in "Come Out!" Newsletter)

Darryl W. Bullock: "The Velvet Mafia: The gay men who ran the swinging sixties" (Book) 2021

George Miller. "The magical number seven, plus or minus two" (Article) 1956

Abraham Maslow: "Hierarchy of Needs" (Article) 1943

Association of Black Psychologists: (https://abpsi.org/about-abpsi/) (Website)

Alan Watts: "The Way of Zen" (Book) 1957

Alan Watts: "Drugs: Turning the head or turning on" (Podcast "Being in the way" episode 7)

Alan Watts: https://alanwatts.org/ (Website)

Ram Dass: "Be Here Now" (Book) 1970

Bibliography

Ram Dass: https://beherenownetwork.com/ (Website)

Ken Kesey: "One flew over the cuckoo's nest" (Book) 1962

Ken Kesey: "Sometimes a great notion" (Book) 1964

Tom Wolfe: "The Electric Kool-Aid Acid Test" (Book) 1968

Richard Neville & Martin Sharp: "Oz" (Newspaper) 1967

John Hopkins, David Mairowitz, Roger Hutchinson, Peter Stansill, Barry Miles, Jim Haynes and Tom McGrath. "IT" (Newspaper) 1967

Hunter s Thompson: "Hashbury" (Article in New York Times) 1967

Newsweek: "Dropouts on a mission" (Magazine article) 1967

Time: "Love on Height" (Magazine article) 1967

Allen Cohen & Michael Bowen: "The Oracle of the City of San-Francisco" (Magazine) 1967

Timothy Leary: "Flashbacks: A personal and cultural history of an era" (Book) 1983

CND Movement: https://cnduk.org/ (Website)

The Bulletin of The Atomic Scientists: https://thebulletin.org/ (Website)

Annie Jacobsen: "Nuclear War, a Scenario" (Book) 2024

Vincent Bugliosi: "Helter Skelter" (Book) 1974

Richard Dawkins: "God Delusion" (Book) 2006

Richard Dawkins: "The Selfish Gene" (Book) 1976

Christopher Hitchens: "God is not Great, how religion poisons everything" (Book) 2007

Alex O'Connor/ Cosmic Skeptic: https://youtube.com/@cosmicskeptic?si=d6_cPe6qOnw1oKSk

YouTube channel and Podcast series "Within Reason"

Scientific & Medical Network: https://scientificandmedical.net/ (Website)

Fritjof Capra: "The Tao Of Physics: An exploration of the parallels between modern physics and Eastern mysticism" (Book) 1975

Donald Hoffman: https://sites.socsci.uci.edu/~ddhoff/ (Website)

Hanna Rosin: "The End Of Men" (Book) 2012

Gabor Maté: https://drgabormate.com/ (Website) (He is a renowned speaker, and bestselling author, Dr. Gabor Maté is highly sought after for his expertise on a range of topics including addiction, stress and childhood development.)

Kati Morton: https://youtube.com/@katimorton?si=c0KMb1eBxbsdZQYc (YouTube. Licenced therapist, author and public speaker)

Dr. Scott Eilers: https://youtube.com/@drscotteilers?si=JI710PvCborjGPI7

(YouTube. Clinical psychologist, Podcast host, and Author of: "For when everything is burning down".)

Gabi Kovalenko: https://youtube.com/@gabikovalenko?si=Yu-wax75n6w9b_ZB (YouTube channel) (Inspiring motivational channel)

T&H – Inspiring and motivational: https://youtube.com/@tradgedyandhope?si=EJJd182dOG3tcdZU (YouTube channel) (Inspiring videos and profound philosophy)

André Duqum: "Know Thyself" (YouTube channel) (Inspiring motivational channel) (Inspiring channel, questioning society and motivational) (Inspiring channel, questioning society and motivational)

Chris Williamson: "Modern Wisdom" https://youtube.com/@chriswillx?si=y-MVlSRxdseQFO9w

(YouTube channel) (Inspiring channel, questioning society and motivational)

Triggernometry: https://youtube.com/@triggerpod?si=Rx9yzvxSK2YtvPJL (YouTube channel) (Inspiring channel, questioning society and motivational)

Big Think: https://youtube.com/@bigthink?si=pKZklZ-ZWouxKAR4 (YouTube channel) (Inspiring channel, educational content and motivational)

Tom Bilyeu: https://youtube.com/@tombilyeu?si=Pivkx6iDhCnVoi77 (YouTube channel) (Inspiring channel, questioning society and motivational)

Steven Bartlett: "The Diary of a CEO": https://youtube.com/@thediaryofaceo?si=sK2dSFrmrfi7pf73 (YouTube channel) (Inspiring channel, questioning society and motivational)

Philip Goff: "Galileo's Error: Foundations for a new science of consciousness" (Book) 2019

Philip Goff: "Why? The purpose of the universe" (Book) 2023

Philip Goff: "Mind chat" (Podcast series)

Ed Winters: "This is Vegan Propaganda" (Book) 2022

Ed Winters: "How to argue with a meat eater (And Win Every Time)" (Book) 2023

Ed Winters: https://youtube.com/@ed.winters?si=sdmCZGLeAYL2Z_mY (Earthling Ed YouTube channel)

Brenda Sanders: https://www.afrovegansociety.org/meet-brenda (Website) (Afro-vegan society website)

Jordan Peterson: "12 Rules for Life" (Book) 2018

Victor Emil Frankl: "Man's Search for Meaning" (Book) 1945

About the Author

Chris Jarmain.

I was born and currently live in the UK, I have encountered many life challenges over the many years I have been alive. As a child, I was diagnosed with Autism, dyslexia, other learning difficulties and sequential memory disorder. The school system advised me and my family that I wouldn't make it in life much further than a trolley attendant for a supermarket.

These issues resulted in my failing school or getting poor results from my GCSEs. I went on to learn in adult education, and remained in self education and formed a perseverance to learn as much as I could, all in the face of adversity. I have since become a fully qualified HGV technician and have gained a reasonable reputation within the motor trade, far removed from the prospect of becoming a trolley attendant.

I have always had a fascination with society and how people work or operate, as I knew I didn't 'work' or 'operate' properly myself, thus I wanted to learn more about myself and how I fit into our society. Because of my childhood, I wanted a more peace loving world in my adult life, hence I was drawn to the 60s era and the Hippie subcultures, because many of their ideals, and or ways of living life held the same narratives I wanted to foster for myself. Since life itself has happened and many issues occurred in my later adult years, I have attempted to take my own life three times. These situations have profoundly shifted my sense of self but have really kicked my desire to pursue the things in life that inspire me, to help others achieve a life of purpose, fulfilment and meaning has become part of that inner shift. I now want to help other people reach a potential that they can be proud of, in essence, I want to help others become masters of their potential, instead of victims of their history. Because of my own life experiences, I know and understand the damaging effects of living a life of victimhood. For most of my life, I have been a victim of myself, others and of society at large, but this has since changed. The insights that come with change are what I am keen on sharing with others.

I became an author in the face of dyslexia and other learning difficulties, my own life has become a part of this realisation and actualisation towards a more fulfilling, meaningful and purposeful life in and of itself, it has become a foundation to reflect upon and help others. I wanted to express these many views of dealing with unavoidable suffering, but to also express the many unique viewpoints my life has given to me. By writing about them, I hope that these insights can positively help others.

I want to write books that inspire the mind and spirit, to challenge certain negative perspectives and help others understand the world around us. I hope my books will speak to you the reader about a story of life that is led by meaning, fulfilment and purpose.

You can find me on:

Wix Blog posts:
https://www.mobileapp.app/to/hxalTrS?ref=cl (Masters Of Destiny)

Instagram:
https://www.instagram.com/chrisj250.cj?igsh=MXA0Y2JoNGM5NnJtbA==
@CHRISJ250.CJ

Facebook:
https://www.facebook.com/profile.php?id=100091729713134

Chris Jarmain Author